UNLOCKED:
the power of you

UNLOCKED: the power of you

GEZIM GASHI

Published by The Self-Publishing Agency Inc.

Copyright © 2021 by Gezim Gashi

First Edition

PAPERBACK ISBN 978-1-954233-13-3
HARDCOVER ISBN 978-1-954233-15-7
EBOOK ISBN 978-1-954233-14-0

All rights reserved under International and Pan-American Copyright Conventions.

Manufactured in Canada.

No part of this publication may be reproduced, stored in or introduced into a retrieval system, or transmitted in any form or by any means (electronic, mechanical, photocopying, recording or otherwise) without the prior written permission of the publisher. This book is sold subject to the condition that it shall not, by way of trade or otherwise, be lent, resold, hired out, or otherwise circulated without the publisher's prior written consent in any form of binding, cover, or condition other than that in which it was published.

AUTHOR BIO Anna Mullens
COVER AND TEXT DESIGN Jazmin Welch (fleck creative studio)
EDITOR Lori Bamber
PUBLISHING SUPPORT TSPA The Self-Publishing Agency Inc.

*To my parents,
Beqir and Hava Gashi*

Table of Contents

- 9   Introduction

  CHAPTER 1
- 11   The Power of Your Story

  CHAPTER 2
- 21   The Power of You

  CHAPTER 3
- 41   The Power of Moments

  CHAPTER 4
- 53   The Power of Yes; The Power of No

  CHAPTER 5
- 75   The Power of a Dream

  CHAPTER 6
- 91   The Power of Play & Passion

  CHAPTER 7
- 101   The Power of Authentic Presence and Connection

  CHAPTER 8
- 115   The Power of Resilience

  CHAPTER 9
- 129   The Power of Creative Collaboration

  CHAPTER 10
- 139   The Power of Why

  CHAPTER 11
- 155   Your Mission: Be the Kindest Person in the Room

- 161   Chapter Forever

Introduction

In so many ways, I've lived what people have called "a charmed life."

As I write this book, I'm thirty, and I'm living my dreams. I run my own company and am a partner in an entertainment high school institute in Los Angeles. I've met and spent time with more astronomically talented performers than my fourteen-year-old self knew existed. Some are my closest friends.

However, when the pandemic hit, everything came to a stop for me, just as it probably did for you and most of the other almost eight billion people on the planet. I realized that, while I'm so grateful for the impact we're able to have on our students, I wanted to share what I've learned with more people.

The world is changing so fast. In many ways, there has never been a better time to be an amateur. What used to take twelve years of post-secondary education to learn can now be done in seconds with an app. At the same time, so much of what used to work for people and business no longer does. The world has moved on, and some of the most experienced people have been left behind.

I realized that the skills and lessons I've learned—I call them my superpowers—are exactly what we *all* need to find our way and thrive in this uncharted territory.

We cannot know what technology will appear tomorrow, the next TikTok or what streaming service will replace YouTube. We don't know what will replace the jobs taken by robotics or even what it will mean to "work" in the next few decades.

Yet, there are abilities that can prepare us for whatever the future holds—because we know the right questions to ask and how to connect with the right people.

Because we know who we are and what we bring to the world.

Thinking about the amazing people that taught me these lessons and skills—from my parents and family to educationalists such as Dr. Jim and Mary Kay Altizer, to entertainment giants like Rami Yacoub and Quincy Jones III—inspired me to write this book.

I've been so fortunate, I know, and while I wish that could be true of every person on Earth, I also know it's not.

By putting this book into the world, the essence of everything I've learned so far about living our best life today and in the world to come, I'm hoping I can tip that balance just a little bit.

Chapter 1

The Power of Your Story

The story you tell yourself about you and your life will determine so much of everything that happens to you afterward.

Consider, for example, Arlind's story.

In 1990, Arlind was born in Prishtina, the capital city of Kosovo. Prishtina and the Balkan states that surround it are a crossroads, a naturally beautiful, historic region. For thousands of years, it is here that Europe met Asia and Islam met Christianity. While people of many ancestries have prospered and lived together peacefully here, its ancient soil is soaked in the blood of countless wars and genocides.

After one of these wars, the most recent, a United Nations–administered Supreme Court determined that there had been a campaign of terror that included "murders, rapes, arsons and severe maltreatments" against the Albanian population, Arlind's people.

Investigators recovered the bodies of more than 3,000 victims; by 1999, more than a million ethnic Albanians had been driven from the region.

Three days after Arlind was born, Kosovo was declared a republic. Although all celebrated the declaration, it also triggered age-old ethnic divisions among extremists.

An Albanian nurse in the largely Yugoslavian-staffed hospital where Arlind was born came to his young mother, Alira, to tell her that a genocide was underway, even within the hospital. The nurse said that Albanian babies were being given injections formulated to make them sick and kill them. Mothers were not being allowed to leave the hospitals with their babies.

There was no way to know if the nurse was right, but rumors had been swirling for months. Alira had to trust her. The alternative—to not trust her and find out she was telling the truth—was unthinkable.

Arlind had been born healthy and emanating happiness. Alira told him later that she knew he was exceptional from the moment she first held him in her arms because he was so calm. She said there was a special sort of energy about him that made her calmer, too, and convinced her that it would all be okay despite everything that was going on.

After talking to the nurse, Alira did the only thing she could think of to save her child.

She telephoned her brother, who was driving from their village with her husband. She told them to come to the hospital and stand outside her second-floor room. Once her brother, the most athletic person in the family, was positioned underneath, Alira leaned out the window as far as she could without falling herself and then dropped the tiny, swaddled infant into his arms. The men ran back to the car with the baby, and Alira dressed and left the hospital.

When the soldiers stopped her at the entrance, she pointed to the store across the street and told them she was going to get a snack. They allowed her to leave, and she met her family a few blocks away. They escaped the city, the center of the unrest, and headed back to their village.

Near their home, they met Alira's mother-in-law on the road, walking back from a neighbor's house. They pulled over to pick her up and tell her what had happened. She climbed into the back seat, and Alira passed the baby to her.

After hearing the story, the grandma said, in Albanian, "This child fills me with happiness. This is the happiest day of my life—Kosovo is a republic, and this child is safe and so special. His name should be Arlind." (Arlind means "born from gold" in Albanian.)

His parents agreed, and the baby became Arlind. As he grew up, he felt that his name was more than just his name. It was a beautiful symbol, a regular reminder of the story that his family told him over and over: he survived genocide and a fall out of a second-floor window because he was special.

He was essential to his family and the world, and he had a purpose to fulfil.

Because of this story, Arlind grew up to be fearless. He was absolutely certain that he would do something special with his life, something no one before or after him could do.

He grew up believing that, like him, each person has a singular destiny—our job is to "keep throwing ourselves at the world" until we find our right path.

"I think I was eight when I went in front of my class and told this story," he says. "I said that I was going to move to the U.S. and do something great; that I was going to make Swedish history.

"The other kids didn't know how to react—afterwards, there was this distance. But our music teacher, Harriett, who sadly passed away a few years ago, was my first mentor outside of my home. From her, I got the message that I could speak and be free, that whenever I had dreams and talked about them, she would be there to applaud for me."

The Story of Lefter

Arlind's best friend in primary school, Lefter, was also born in an Albanian family in Kosovo.

By the time the two boys reached kindergarten, their families had fled to the same small Swedish town as refugees.

But the story Lefter heard about himself was different.

Named after a famous football star, Lefter felt he'd disappointed his father because he wasn't at all interested in sports. He loved music and any new technology that allowed him to share it with others.

From the native Swedes in his small town, he often heard how lucky he was to live in Sweden, to have escaped the horrors of the war in Kosovo. From his Swedish friends, he heard, "Lefter, you are a refugee, but you are a good refugee."

In 1995, when his family became Swedish citizens, he struggled because he didn't feel Swedish.

"I think that's something that all refugees go through," he said as an adult. "Kosovo declared peace in 1999, so we still lived with the war until then, even if we were in Sweden. We didn't know what was happening with my family. And I heard all the time that I was so fortunate, that I should be grateful—what else could I want?"

Lefter grew up wanting to do what his teachers, friends and parents thought he should: choose the safest path. He didn't want to cause any more worry for his family. He went to a technical school and became a software engineer. He married early and stayed in the small town where his parents lived.

But at night, after his family was asleep, he played the music that he loved and felt a strange sense of longing. Sometimes, for no reason he could describe, he found himself resenting his family and the people he worked with.

Your Story, Your Choice

These stories, of Arlind and Lefter, are true. In some of their details, they are also fiction.

"Arlind" is me—I was that baby, tossed from that window, and my parents raised me to believe I could do anything with my life. I grew up knowing it to be true. I never doubted it. Even now, when things go wrong, as they sometimes do, I know that I only need to find my way back to the right path.

Lefter is also me, or, at least, Lefter is the person I might have become were it not for my parents and the story they told me about who I am.

From the people outside my family, I often heard that I was so lucky to be a refugee in Sweden, that I should be grateful and not reach too high or ask for too much. I was, after all, not Swedish—I'm a dark-haired man in a country of blonds. My family had nothing, no wealth or connections that might have convinced others I would do anything other than survive and live quietly through the years I'd been granted. Who did I think I was to dream so big?

Because of my parents, because of their focus on my story, I never really heard those people. It didn't even occur to me that not having wealth or connections, living in a small town and being a refugee would be real barriers. I believed I'd find a way, like my mom did.

I was so convinced that, when a television station in a nearby city announced that they were looking for special local stories, I called up Gunilla Hellgren, the producer, and told her I was ready for my interview.

She asked why they should interview me. "I live in Alvesta [a small town in the south of Sweden] and am a fourteen-year-old Albanian refugee from Kosovo. Despite that, I have big dreams, and I think that is a special story."

After thinking about it for a while, she said, "But we'll be in Alvesta Thursday morning. You'll be in school?"

"No," I said. "I'm off that day."

I wasn't off that day.

On Thursday morning, I went to school, Grönkullaskolan, as usual. When it was time for the interview, I told the teacher I had to go to the bathroom. I left the school and went home. When I walked in our front door, my mother asked me what I was doing there, why I wasn't at school.

"A TV reporter is coming to interview me here. I told my teacher I was going to the bathroom, but I left. You should make coffee."

My mom has always believed in me, but I think that was the moment when she was like, "You know, you can do whatever you want. I can see the fire in your eyes. You'll be fine."

Gezim means joy and happiness in Albanian, and it is the name my grandmother bestowed on me a few hours after my mother threw me out of that second-floor window.

I am here to bring people joy, and entertainment became my first platform. I've been consulting as a producer for TV programs since 2006. In 2009, I graduated from the Media-TV/Radio program at Kungsmadskolan in Växjö. I went on to produce content for Swedish TV channels such as SVT and TV4. I was one of the producers for the reality show, "Music Academy," and for "The Club" and "Soy Luna" on Disney Channel Scandinavia.

In 2018, after working with students at music schools in Sweden for several years, I partnered with Oaks Christian School to launch a high school institute for the entertainment industry in Los Angeles, the OCS Institute of Arts and Innovation. Offering pathways in songwriting, music production, film, dance, visual arts and acting, the institute prepares students for careers in entertainment and for acceptance in the leading art colleges in the U.S.

In early 2020, before the pandemic, I was even invited to speak at Harvard University about my journey.

Working with dozens of incredibly talented students along the way, I've come to understand that the stories we tell ourselves about ourselves are the bedrock of true confidence, the kind that comes from knowing we are here to do something meaningful with our lives. Listening to those who lack that confidence tell me about the many ways in which they aren't special, I realized that my story had become a superpower.

Arlind is me; Lefter is the person most of us will become if we let other people tell us our stories. I was fortunate—my parents gifted me with a perception of myself that had no limits. But if you aren't lucky in this way, and most people aren't, it doesn't matter. Your story is yours to choose.

It is up to you to find it, and once you do, to wear it like a crown and a shield. It is your limitless battery pack.

I call it our superpower story, the one that reminds us who we are and what we're here for when we forget.

According to the brilliant social researcher Brené Brown, human beings are primed for story—story is the way we learn, grow and connect. This is true in our relationships with others, but it is also true in our relationship with ourselves. If you want to unlock the power of you—to arm yourself with genuine authenticity and confidence—first unlock your story.

I've done my best to make it easy in the next chapter.

Chapter 2

The Power of You

Susan Cain, the best-selling author of *Quiet, The Power of Introverts in a World that Can't Stop Talking,* writes that our story is the narrative we have constructed from the events of our life.

In an article she wrote for *Psychology Today* magazine, (and which appears on her website, The Quiet Revolution), she asks, "What is your story? **And do you know that this is the single most important question you can ask yourself?**"

It isn't difficult to begin to write your superpower story, no matter what you've learned about yourself until now.

Think for a moment about how many of your ancestors had to survive long enough to have a child for you to be here. (Um, all of them!) You come from a long line of people who survived enormous predators, wars, famines and oppression long enough to have a child. Amazing!

Then, after all those unlikely survivals, your parents had to connect to have you. Out of more than seven billion other people in the world, they had to find each other. Think about the incredible odds of one sperm cell reaching one egg to make you the person you are, and not your sister or your brother!

The chances of you being born are astronomically small.

Beyond the absolute miracle that is your existence, your combination of DNA and environmental influences is totally unique. You have a blend of talents that exists in only one being in the world.

You.

There is something that only you are ideally suited to do. But what is? How do you find it?

I hear you.

If you feel more like Lefter than like Arlind, your purpose in life right now is to write your own superpower story. Even if you feel more like Arlind, it's useful to revisit and articulate your story just to ensure it's as powerful as it can be.

The Building Blocks of Your Superpower Story

Every story is a composite of characters, setting and events. There is conflict, and there is conflict resolution.

Many people tell their story more or less chronologically, as I did in the Arlind story: I was born, I grew up, this happened along the way, now I am here. Focus also on your turning points, those moments in your life when you learned something new about yourself that changed what you did afterwards. It is in the turning points that we find our conflicts and our resolutions. Yours is not a short story—it is an epic. Like the protagonists in *War and Peace*, you will experience many critical turning points. (I like to remember a meme that I came across online that goes something like: "Never forget you've solved 100 percent of the problems you've experienced until now.")

For me, one of those turning points was my first TV interview at age fourteen—making that crazy call told me a lot about what was possible, what I was capable of, and what I wanted from life.

If we believe we are unlucky, we are less likely to take the measured risks that allow good things to happen in our lives. If we believe that we are ordinary, we will look to other people to tell us how we should live.

If we feel we are unworthy, we will find ways to avoid all the good things coming our way.

If we believe we can grow and learn from challenges, we are so much more likely to take on new challenges and succeed.

Remember: To be ordinary means to be wholly unique and special in a world of wholly unique and special humans. No one can tell you how to be you. You're the first, the only. You are the inventor, the architect and the conductor of your world.

If you're building a business, advice from successful business owners can be helpful, but advice from doctors probably wouldn't be. Similarly, advice from great communicators may help you learn excellent communication skills—but it will rarely get you any closer to **knowing who you are and what you have to offer the world.**

Your Superpower: Telling the Story of You

Before we go any further together, I want you to write your superpower story.

Here is a process that can make it easier. But plan on spending at least a few hours on this over a couple of weeks. And know that you will reach your maximum superpower-story strength over a lifetime of learning more about yourself—this is an exercise you should do at least once a year.

You'll need a notebook with pages large enough to draw a timeline across two facing pages that includes every year of your life up until now. (See pages 28 and 29.)

STEP 1

Across two pages of your notebook, create a timeline from your birth until today. Now intersect the timeline with events and the places in which those events happened. (Remembering place will help you remember the associated emotions, not just the bare bones.)

For example, say you were born in 1988 in San Diego, just after your grandfather died. In 1993, you started kindergarten in Newton where you met your first best friend, Lily. You stepped on a nail at summer camp at Lake Lavoie in 1997 and had to go home. You failed French in grade 6 in Newton (2000); you developed a massive crush on Trina down the street that summer. In 2002, your next-door neighbor gave you his old violin, and you practiced relentlessly until your parents told you they couldn't stand it anymore and bought you a guitar.

To squeeze in as much as possible, use numbers to represent events on the timeline. Use another page in your notebook to write a list of the numbered events with as much detail as you'd like. Here is an example of what it will end up looking like.

STEP 2

Create a new section in your notebook, and using your numbered list, write about each event and what it taught you about yourself and life.

This exercise is the character development part of your story. Who is the hero, and what makes them tick?

You're looking for everything that makes you, you—what are you good at, what are you not so good at, what do you love and dislike? What do people respond to about you when they're with you? What do you do when you want to cheer someone up? What are you most likely to do when you're frustrated?

Humans are complicated; there is no question. We are all composites of our inherited characteristics (the ones that come embedded in our DNA), our environment, our predispositions and our choices. It can be difficult to put words to these concepts.

Born

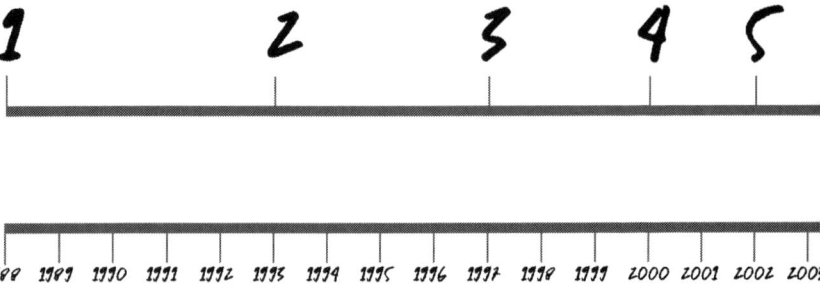

Now

2006 2007 2008 2009 2010 2011 2012 2013 2014 2015 2016 2017 2018 2019 2020 2021

1. I was born in 1988, just after grandpa died; my dad was very depressed in those first two years.

2. In 1993, I started kindergarten and met Lily, who has been my best friend ever since.

3. 1997: I stepped on a nail at camp and have to go home. I learned that bad things happened and I became afraid I was accident-prone.

4. 2000: Fell hard for Trina. She broke my heart.

5. 2002: Jon next door gave me his old violin. I played it until may parents bought me a guitar so they wouldn't have to listen to the vionlin. I learned that music is my main form of expression.

6.

7.

8.

9.

10.

11.

12.

13.

14.

15.

16.

17.

18.

19.

20.

Here are some labels that can help. Try them on, almost like you would t-shirts with logos and memes on them. Using each word, make three lists in your notebook:

1. This fits.
2. This fits but isn't comfortable—it's a stretch.
3. This doesn't fit.

Let's start with what we value:

Perseverance
Loyalty   Positivity
Adventure **Compassion**
Commitment
Dependability   Motivation
Open-mindedness
Efficiency
Fitness **Honesty**
Creativity
Environmentalism   Consistency
Good humor
Service to others   Education
Optimism
Reliability
Courage
Passion
Respect Innovation

Here are some commonly used labels for character traits. Which of these would you use to describe yourself? Have others used any of these words to describe you?

Cooperative

Tolerant

Faithful Fair

Generous

Patient **Self-controlled**

Has Integrity Loyal

Optimistic Loving

Devoted

Peaceful **Persistent**

Sincere

Determined Spiritual

Kind

People high on the agreeableness factor may also be:

- Compassionate
- Congenial
- Cooperative
- Empathetic
- Friendly
- Good-natured
- Gracious
- Pleasant
- Trusting

People who are conscientious may also be considered:

- Dutiful
- Exact
- Faithful
- Mindful
- Steadfast
- Truthful

Extroverts may also be described as:

- Affable
- Companionable
- Convivial
- Gregarious
- Outgoing
- Sociable

People who are considered open may also be:

- Accepting
- Broad-minded
- Daring
- Insightful
- Receptive
- Tolerant

Neuroticism is a category that describes the traits in us that can make life more difficult for us or the people around us. To some degree or another, in some way or another, we are all neurotics. As the early psychologist Carl Jung put it, neurosis is unresolved tension between the unconscious and the ego—in other words, the outward manifestation of something we're working on.

Various neurotic behaviors can be described this way:

- Agitated
- Angry
- Anxious
- Depressed
- Impatient
- Jittery
- Sensitive
- Tense
- Uneasy

Until we get to neuroticism, the labels above are considered positive. We are all doing our best, but under stress, we often display traits that are less than effective at helping us achieve our best life.

Rather than adopting these labels for ourselves as our "dark side" or our flaws, it can be helpful to reach for them to describe what is most likely to happen to us when we're triggered or feel overwhelmed.

These "negative" characteristics are often just the intensification of our "positive" traits that happens when we're under extreme stress. For example, someone who is very honest and forthright is also probably more likely to be viewed as unkind, rude, abrasive or even cruel when they're under pressure and don't have time to think.

Think about the last time you really lost it on someone. Would any of these labels apply?

As a side note, it's helpful to remember that when we apply these labels to others, it's often their behavior under stress that we're describing, not who they are as people.

Rude
Abrasive Caustic
Disrespectful
Cruel
Selfish Unkind
Mean Greedy
Dishonest
Narcissistic
Unforgiving Disloyal
Obnoxious
Malicious Impatient
Quarrelsome
Petty Pessimistic
Unmerciful

Now that you've tried these words on, describe your hero for someone who hasn't met them[1].

- What makes them, them?
- What are they better at than most people?
- What bores them?
- What excites them?
- What do they admire in other people?
- What do they fear in other people?
- What gets them out of bed in the morning?
- What do they do when they're sad or hurt?
- What do they do when someone else is sad or hurt?
- What do they most look forward to doing at work?
- What do their friends love about them?
- What do their colleagues appreciate about them?
- What do their family members love about them, and become frustrated with?

Now that you've described the hero of your story, it's up to you to figure out what brings out the best, the mediocre and the worst in you.

What will equip you to become your best self in the future?

---

[1] Notice that I'm slipping between "you" and "they," you the person reading and "they," your fictional superhero who is also you. This is an easy tool to use to stimulate insights about yourself. Whenever you get stuck, imagine yourself as a comic book hero.

Chapter 3

The Power of Moments

I can't remember how old I was when I first understood that I was meant to do something special in my life. I know I was still a young child, just looking at myself in my mirror, and it became clear. Nothing would stop me.

I will never forget that moment because even though nothing exceptional was going on, it turned into a memory that still drives me to take risks and reach higher. It was on my mind when I called the TV4 producer and told her they should come interview me.

In a way, the entire book you hold in your hand is the product of a series of singular moments, big and little, snapshots that showed me who I am and what I'm meant for.

The term "aha moment" was included in the *Merriam-Webster Dictionary* for the first time in 2012. The announcement was accompanied by a video featuring the person who made it part of our popular culture, Oprah.

In the video, she describes an aha moment as a moment of insight. But later, she added something fascinating to her definition during an interview with Harry Connick, Jr. You cannot have an aha moment, she said, about something you don't already know.

The moment is not teaching you something—instead it helps you remember something you have forgotten or haven't been able to articulate.

A friend of mine describes these moments as messages from her higher self. She tells the story of just standing by her fridge, replaying a conflict she was having with someone at work in her mind. A "small, quiet voice" said, "You are trying to convince yourself that you are better than other people because you feel that you do not belong."

It took a while for her to figure out what that message meant, but it eventually changed everything for her. She realized that her tendency to try to be "the best" was moving her **away** from what she really wanted: a community of like-minded people and work that helped others. She'd built her life around achieving things like the right title and salary, and she worked in an industry that focused almost solely on making money.

From that moment forward, she thought less about the next promotion and more about surrounding herself with people with similar values. That meant leaving her job as an executive and taking significant financial risks to become a writer. It meant leaving her marriage to someone with entirely different values.

Slowly, one step at a time, she created a life that was hers. And it all started with one moment beside the fridge—such an ordinary moment.

I also felt this way when I met my friends and mentors, Jim and Mary Kay, who I write about a lot, later in the book.

It was just a meeting.

They wanted to learn more about our school; I wanted to show them the outstanding accomplishments of our students. But almost instantly, I knew there was a deep connection between us, and I could immediately see the potential for a powerful partnership.

Speaking at Harvard

Other moments were more recognizably memorable at the time.

When I was invited to speak at Harvard University in March 2020, I brought my mother and sister.

As we walked to the auditorium on campus, we passed many posters featuring my photo. My sister asked my mom to stand beside one so she could take a photo. In that moment, all my earlier aha moments felt like lamps on the path that had led me toward this lifelong dream.

I thought about how it must feel for my mom to remember dropping me out of that hospital window to save my life and then watching me speak at Harvard—I was so grateful and proud that I could give her that joy.

Moments can be catalysts, but the reason most of the moments we remember are dramatically great or dramatically bad is that those are the ones that capture our attention. The problem with this phenomenon is that most of the truly life-changing insights we have are more like my moment looking in the mirror or my friend's moment at her fridge and less like my moment at Harvard.

The idea that the most critical moments are exceptional is dangerous in that it keeps us chasing the highs, following important people around or scrolling through Instagram to see what our favorite influencers are doing.

So how can we have more of the aha moments that show us the way forward? First, we must learn to **be** in the moment.

In his book *Waking Up: A Guide to Spirituality Without Religion*, neuroscientist Sam Harris writes, "How we pay attention to the present moment largely determines the character of our experience and, therefore, the quality of our lives." In another segment of the same book, he says, "My mind begins to seem like a video game: I can either play it intelligently, learning more in each round, or I can be killed in the same spot by the same monster, again and again."

Learning more in each round means inhabiting the moments we're in, and in many ways, this has never been harder to do. Just tell yourself you're not going to check your phone for an hour. Then count the times you think about checking your phone. Scary, right?

Insight is a bit like sleep. We can't make it happen. We don't know how. All we can do is prepare space for it and show up. Regrettably, this is not a one-size-fits-all exercise. We all have different needs when it comes to making space for insight, for making it more likely that we won't be killed in the same spot by the same monster. Many people say they do their best thinking in the shower, or late at night, or on walks in the forest. The reason that insights come to us at these moments is that we are not chasing them—we're creating space for them to come to us at a time we're present enough to receive them.

It isn't hard to find out what works best for you when it comes to creating this space. Let's do that right now.

Mapping the Moments that Lift You Up

On your timeline, add the events that might be considered aha moments in your life.

Map them beside the particularly happy moments, the sad and angry moments, the frightening moments.

Include events that helped you build new strengths and uncover talents you didn't know you had. Make sure you've included the worst moments of your life so far, and the best.

Now think about each event. Ask yourself what your hero's purpose is in that moment. Are you learning, contributing to the world, discovering new strengths, having an insight, facing a challenge you didn't think you'd be able to face? Creating new art to help people feel and understand the world? Teaching others new skills? Are there moments in which you decided not to face the challenge in front of you and decided instead to blame the problem on someone else— or escaped into distractions like drugs or alcohol? Did those moments give you more compassion for others and teach you lessons about what it means to be a human under stress?

Think about things that your hero once believed but doesn't any longer, and about what they were wrong about that held them back.

The past cannot tell you who you are, but it can give you clues about which future will provide you with the most freedom to be entirely yourself.

Now make three new lists in your notebook.

1. Moments that taught you something important.
2. Challenges that forced you to build new strengths.
3. Events that were milestones, that represent the beginning of a new chapter in your life story. (Even if you didn't think about it that way at the time.)

Once you've listed these moments, think about what they had in common. What kind of people were with you? How often were you alone when you had new insights? Where were you?

If you were writing a superhero comic with you as the lead superhero, what kind of characters would you surround them with? Who brings out their best and appreciates them?

What kind of environments do they thrive in? Do they do their best work when they're in a group of creative people or alone in their room? Do they seek out complete quiet to study or do their best work in coffee shops? Are they more intimidated by people in positions of authority or inspired to learn from them? Do they prefer to invent new ways of doing things or imitate the masters in that field?

Remember, it is up to you to know what makes this superhero thrive and then to provide as many of those elements as possible in the pages to come.

In his posthumously published book *Markings,* the Swedish diplomat and economist Dag Hammarskjöld wrote, "At every moment you choose yourself. But do you choose *your* self? Body and soul contain a thousand possibilities out of which you can build many I's."

He went on to say that there is only one "I" that is the consciousness of the talent you were entrusted with, and that the only way to find it is to cast off everything else.

My dear friend Ulla Sjöström, the founder of Musikmakarna (Songwriters Academy of Sweden), is widely considered the most important woman in the music industry in Sweden. As she said to me, "Do the best thing you can until you know better."

Everything we do is a step towards our best self or away from it, toward some other possible version of ourselves.

Another humble moment, from another friend, who writes:

I was a few weeks sober, and after a twelve-step meeting, I went for coffee with some people from my home group. I felt like I had a new skin—I walked around like life was normal, but everything was so unfamiliar, and I wasn't sure who I was.

At some point, I went to the bathroom, and when I came out of the stall, a young blond woman was washing her hands at the only sink. I waited quietly for her to finish, which took only a moment.

She turned and smiled at me and said, "I left the warm water on for you—it takes a while to warm up here."

And in that moment, I knew who I wanted to be in the world. I wanted to be someone so present in my own life that I would notice the person standing behind me and remember to leave the warm water on for them.

That moment encapsulated everything that was wrong with my life to that point and everything I was aiming to build and become.

In this story, this almost comically humble moment—in a bathroom, at a sink—becomes a symbol for a whole set of values.

In many ways, the gesture my friend remembers, someone just leaving the warm water on for her, is the epitome of what Buddhists call being a Bodhisattva. A Bodhisattva is committed to the development of emotional clarity and focus so great that they are entirely present to others.

Bodhisattvas are not worried about what they should be doing or what others think of them. They're not thinking about their next move. They are simply there, ready to receive other people and offer them whatever comfort they can.

While the concept is simple, it is the work of a lifetime. Daily effort is required to still our mind and become present. It can take years to overcome the insecurities that have us looking around us at others, hoping they will tell us who we are.

As long as we are doing that work, however, whenever we meet other people, we meet heart-to-heart. And when we meet heart-to-heart, magic will happen for us and those around us.

What is the work? Simply learning to be present in the moment, first when we are alone and then also when we are with other people.

Mindfulness meditation is one way to develop this skill, and perhaps it is even the best way. But we all know what it means to be mindful—it's when we're carried away on a dancefloor, sweating and tired but completely entranced by the music and light. It's when we're making love to someone we care for deeply or when we are halted on a walk by the beauty of a sunset.

We all have those glorious moments. Becoming present requires that we make it a priority to have more of them.

Finally, a little gift for you to take with you into the future.

Get quiet and comfortable, and close your eyes. Imagine you're walking through a forest. You can hear the birds twittering and occasionally breaking into song.

The scents of the earth under your feet waft upward, bringing you a kind of alert comfort. You are forest bathing, steeped in the organic compounds released by the living beings around and under you.

With each step, feel your feet connect to the energy of the Earth. You can feel the power of gravity and the love the trees feel for the sun.

Breathe deeply.

Up ahead, you can see the sun shining more brightly. There is a clearing.

Just before you reach it, find a soft patch of moss under a tree, and with your back to the tree, take a comfortable seat.

Take your mind back in time to a moment when life was good, and you were entirely at ease. It may have been a moment just after you woke up, before your thoughts found you. Or lying on a beach, pretending you were still asleep while your friends played around you.

Don't worry about experimenting with a few different memories. But eventually, when you return to a place where you were completely comfortable and at ease, stay there for a few minutes.

When new thoughts try to steal you away, just watch them come and go before moving back to this place of ultimate comfort.

See what arises for you. What message does this moment have for you? Wait until something surprises you.

You can't prepare for aha moments—many of the most important will come to you at unexpected times. But the more you practice this small exercise, this gift to yourself, the more likely you are to be awake for the insight when it comes.

And that, my friend, can change everything.

Chapter 4

The Power of Yes; The Power of No

"If you aren't working on Saturdays and Sundays, someone else will, and they are going to take your seat."
—**DAVID FOSTER**

I met David a few years ago at Universal Music Group in Los Angeles, where he did a master class for my students. He has long been an inspiration to me, and it was amazing to meet with him and watch him teach our students.

One of the things he said, something that I'll never forget, is quoted above.

Unless we identify whatever it is that we want to do more than watching Netflix or checking our phone or sleeping in, we won't have the energy and determination needed.

Once you find the thing that you will say yes to, always, it becomes easier to say no to everything else.

We make so many decisions every day. Whether to hit snooze, whether to send that email, whether to reach out and try again to schedule that meeting with the person who seems to be avoiding us. The power of yes, "Yes, I do want to do this thing more than anything else," is the power that keeps us moving forward.

Yes unleashes our energy and our talents.

But it is the power of **no** that frees us to succeed. Without it, the work we do on Saturdays and Sundays may be taking us in the absolute wrong direction.

How many times have you watched people succeed at something only to realize it wasn't really what they wanted? Become the greatest in their field and then fall into despair or self-sabotage?

How many times have you invested time and energy in attracting the attention of a person you later realized wasn't someone you wanted in your life?

As many wise people have said before me, success isn't just about working hard, but about working smart. Stephen R. Covey, the author of the monumental bestseller *The 7 Habits of Highly Effective People*, said, "Management is efficiency in climbing the ladder of success; leadership determines whether the ladder is leaning against the right wall."

It is true of our influence on other people, but even more importantly, it is true of our stewardship of our own lives.

There are so many ways we can allow our time and energy to be drained by unimportant tasks, bad habits and procrastination[2]. Many people are outpaced while working long hours—they aren't working on the right things, or they aren't regularly recharging their energy and so they burn out.

In *The 7 Habits of Highly Effective People,* Covey introduced another life-changing idea: our success is determined largely by how well we care for the people who make us successful. For example, I know that I wouldn't be alive if it weren't for my family—they are the people who make everything I do worthwhile. If I had the choice of being at the Grammys or being with my family, my question would be, "Which would make my family happier?" And that isn't self-sacrifice on my part—my happiness **is** my family's happiness, and their happiness is mine. I can be 100 percent sure that they will want me to do what is best for me. That's what will make them happy. So, success for me includes making time for my family, no matter what. When they need me, I'm there for them.

Similarly, I know that my body and mind are the instruments that enable me to live my best life. Sleeping at least seven hours a night doesn't interfere with my work—it is the foundation of my work, just as Serena Williams eats

---

2 Procrastination can also be a valuable signal we're on the wrong path. Never just assume it's a failure of self-discipline—it may be trying to save your life.

nutritious food and employs the best practice techniques to win championships.

Barack Obama had a closet full of identical blue suits so that he didn't have to think about what to wear. Steve Jobs wore a black turtleneck and jeans to work every day. Many accomplished people eat the same breakfast and lunch each day to remove yet another decision and series of tasks from their schedule.

The healthiest people make activity part of their daily routine.

In his book *Atomic Habits*, James Clear makes a powerful case for the impact of tiny changes, which he compares to the slightest adjustment in a flight path. Initially, the change is almost unnoticeable, which is why it's easier to make. Within a brief time, however, when a change becomes a habit, the impact on your direction and destination is significant.

And all habits are seeded in a yes and a no. Yes to one thing, no to everything else.

Clear and other researchers have found that it is very difficult to stop a bad habit but much easier to replace a bad habit with a positive one.

We say no to having a cigarette or eating that second pastry and yes to going out for a walk while we talk to a friend on the phone. If we deprive ourselves of pleasure, our mind and body will find a way to recalibrate—we want and need pleasure! But if we can replace one kind of pleasure with another, the new pleasure will become a positive habit quickly.

No to one thing, yes to another.

Yes to one thing, no to another.

We get more effective at life and all decisions when we think in terms of this couplet rather than about all the decisions we must make.

Sometimes this balancing act of yes and no is easy and clear. I know that partying until the early morning will cost me my energy and focus the next day; it might even leave me with a fuzzy head a day or two after that if I indulge too much. Being clear on my "yes" makes it easy—yes, I want to help other people identify and leverage their brilliance, which means I don't have any days to waste.

Yes, I have to be sharp.

No, I'm not going to stay at that party past eleven.

Sometimes it's a little harder. I love being with my students and colleagues in LA. But because we couldn't be together in person anyway, I chose to work from home in Sweden during the pandemic lockdowns.

That decision-making process kind of looked like this:

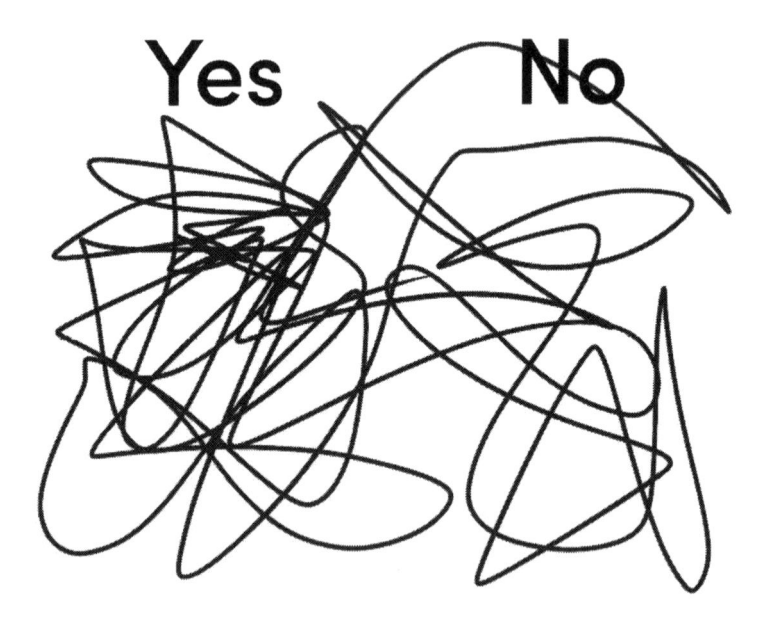

Eventually, though, it became clear for me. It made a lot more sense to be home with my family talking to my students online than it did to be isolated in my LA apartment talking to my students online.

It distilled down to:

Yes: Be with my family while serving my students.
No: Be alone in LA while serving my students.

Sometimes it's a *lot* harder.

The TV4 interview when I was fourteen made me something of a local celebrity, and I told everyone that I was moving to Los Angeles to go to music school after I graduated from high school. I worked hard for two years in a job I did not like to save money, and then I did. It was a big deal in my small town.

I travelled alone to LA. After riding the subway all night long because none of my couch-surfing connections had worked out, I finally found a sketchy but affordable place to stay.

A few days later, I went to the school orientation, which started with a tour. I almost immediately knew it was not right for me.

After the tour, when we were supposed to sign all the registration forms, I told them I needed some time to think. They were shocked. And not happy.

I stepped out of the building onto the Walk of Fame on Hollywood Boulevard. Looking at the stars in the sidewalk going on and on into the distance, I thought, "No, this is not for me."

I walked for a while, and that feeling didn't waver. I went back to the school and told them I wasn't going to attend.

It wasn't until I was writing this book that I realized that, even during that brief tour, I could tell that school's methods were about imposing an understanding of the traditional music world upon us.

I already knew that the music industry they were preparing their students for was dying, and I wanted to prepare for the one that was being born.

In his book *Originals: How Non-Conformists Move the World*, Wharton professor and brilliant management thinker Adam Grant writes that experience improves our ability to make intuitive decisions when the environment we're working in is stable, such as that of doctors.

But in unstable, rapidly changing environments, such as that of political forecasters, experience *reduces* the effectiveness of intuitive decisions.

According to his research, my intuitive understanding was more likely to be accurate than that of the more experienced people at the school.

I didn't know that at the time. All I knew for sure was that it didn't feel right for me. The school and the city were both marketed as a place where dreams come true, and that's where I thought I was going. But when I arrived, I realized that LA is not a pretty place—there is a lot of suffering there.

I had done some media interviews in Sweden before leaving for LA, and I knew what I would face when I went home.

"Yeah, he thinks he's so great—can't even hack it in LA."

"Back in less than a month!"

Yet, I knew that the school didn't align with who I am or what I wanted. It wasn't where I belonged. Sure, part of me said I'd failed at my dream of going to music school in LA. But another part of me held on to my larger dream, the idea that I would find my way forward. I held on to my "yes."

It was a time of rethinking for me, and after arriving back home, I got a job at the electricity company where my brother worked. I started to save more money.

I went back to collaborating with other creative people. I dived into YouTube and the other streaming platforms that I knew would be the future of music and entertainment. I was always running channels where I could highlight and promote other artists.

One of the artists that I connected with, someone who has been a big inspiration since then, is Jeremy Passion. I always listened to his music when I was feeling down because it spoke to me in a way that I can't even explain. When my grandpa died of cancer when I was sixteen, when I was just this kid who really wanted to do well, Jeremy's music healed me. With each failure and loss I've had, I've turned to his music.

When we launched the institute in LA, Jeremy taught our first artist master class and came to perform for the students. It was so moving for me—he sang all the songs that touched me and changed my life. Now he was in front of all these new students of sixteen and fifteen, the same age I was when I found his music.

It was a magical experience, the completion of a circle that began when I'd faced such challenges and found comfort in his music. Now we were *creating* the school programs I had wanted to learn in, all with Jeremy's music as the soundtrack.

Today, in our entertainment industry institute in LA, we teach our students the skills they need for the future, not the past.

Sometimes, applying the power of no means just moving on.

I've had experiences in which people disappointed me, and it can be tempting to be bitter or angry. But as my father taught me, "The best revenge is moving on."

Sometimes, the most potent no is, "I will focus on living my dream without them."

Does it align with and move me toward my dreams? Yes!

Anything else? I'm afraid that's a no.

Viral Yes, Viral No

When I talked to the producer at TV4, I had a very powerful yes, so I didn't give her the power of no. When you ask someone if they are interested in doing something, it's easy for them to say no. When you say, "When are you coming?" as I did, it's much harder.

As I was growing up, my parents had to send a lot of what they earned back to our families in Kosovo, and they were always honest with us about that. There were times we had one T-shirt and one pair of jeans, and we wore them all week. But we knew that our family in Kosovo needed the money more, so we were happy to do it.

When I was fourteen, I heard about Musikhuset, in Växjö, an afterschool organization where creative kids met to sing, record, write music and collaborate on Wednesday evenings. But my family didn't have the money I needed to take the bus there every week.

I knew I had to figure it out on my own.

One day I saw an elderly woman struggling to clean up her garden, and I introduced myself. I told her I needed money for a bus ticket each week, and in return, I would come and fix her garden. I didn't give her time to say no—the next Wednesday, I came back and started work.

Every Wednesday, I went and took care of her garden. Afterwards, she gave me the money I needed for the bus. And she would always have a cinnamon bun and a cherry juice waiting for me. She was sad living alone, and so we would talk. (That's when I began to appreciate the value of just being there for someone and listening to their story.)

I came to understand that everything is an opportunity. There will be barriers. But if you have a powerful yes, you'll find a way to make it happen. A passionate yes makes it very hard for people to say no to you.

Your Yes and No Map

"The sole purpose of human existence is to kindle a light in the darkness of mere being," wrote psychotherapist Carl Jung in his book *Memories, Dreams, Reflections*.

So far, everything you have read is about the process of finding our own light in this sense. What is it we bring to the world?

The problem with life is that it is complicated. We want to be healthy, but we also want to eat that pizza. And that pizza, and that pizza. We want to succeed, but we are so tired. We know this relationship drains our energy and our confidence, but we don't want to be alone. And that day we spent together six months ago was so much fun!

There is only one way through these complications: a powerful yes, and a powerful **no**. This yes/no map creates a framework that turns our yeses into the path of least resistance, the way we turn automatically and without effort.

When you chart your "action steps" in the chapters ahead, you might notice that caring for your instrument (yes, that's you) isn't among the first items you put on your list. In the last two centuries, Westerners have been taught that our bodies are machines and that the best machines need the least care. Now disproven over and over, this false paradigm is part of the world that is dying. The leaders of the future will be those who understand that whole, nourished, energized humans are the world's creative engines.

As an antidote to that dying paradigm, let's create your self-care system first.

What inspires and energizes you?

Think back over the last year or two. Opening your notebook, find a new page and make a list of every experience that lifted you up.

In addition to what you were doing, include the details. Who was there? Where were you, and what about that environment was uplifting? What did you do the day before? What mood were you in to start with, and what mood were you in at the end?

Once you've finished, put this list aside for at least a few days, preferably a week. Then come back to it and make a new list—everything that these experiences had in common.

Feeding You

American writer and philosopher Henry David Thoreau wrote, "The mass of men live lives of quiet desperation."

Why?

Because we get busy paying the bills. And make no mistake, the bills must be paid.

So, how do we do that in the early stages of our professional life? Without accepting a life of quiet desperation, without giving up our vision and letting our lights dim?

Like the woman I describe later in the book who found herself cleaning up after horse surgeries for minimum wage, the key is to unlock our imagination.

Once we do, one of two things will happen. We will find work that energizes us because it allows us to use our talents and passions. Or we will find work that pays well enough that we have time and energy left in each week to devote to our future.

Either way works. You might assume the first is best, but you might be wrong.

Another friend of mine shares her own life as an example. She loves writing, particularly poetry and short stories. But only two or three people in her whole country make a living writing poetry and short stories. So, my friend wrote for magazines and newspapers. She loved it, but she didn't get to decide what she wrote—every article she worked on was assigned to her. It paid well, but it was stressful and exhausting, and she had no time or energy to write the short stories and poetry she loved.

Twenty years passed.

Each year, she made more money, and her lifestyle became more expensive. She spent a fair bit just recovering from the stress of her industry: massage, holidays, costly treats that made her feel a bit better. She gave as much as she could to charities because it was the only way she felt she could contribute. Her health started to fail; first, small things, like too many colds, and then more significant issues, like insomnia and migraines that wouldn't stop.

Eventually, she realized that she had followed her passion right out of the life she really wanted; the stress she had to manage had become chronic burnout. She was just surviving, even though, from the outside, she was very successful in a highly desirable field.

Slowly, she stepped away from all her most expensive habits, including her many health therapies and charitable donations. She shifted her time into supporting her community directly through volunteering, which energized her. She found that, as she began to enjoy the hours of her day more, she just didn't need as much. She downsized her home and life in many ways. A few years later, she was able to focus on the work she wanted to do, she'd reduced her expenses by more than four-fifths and she'd healed her health challenges. Feeding yourself is a simple formula: money in, money out. You can succeed by making more money or spending less money. The point of balance is entirely determined by what you want for your life.

In the 1940s, a woman named Mildred Lisette Norman faced a crisis in her life. Her marriage had failed; she felt that her ordinary, materialistic life had also failed. She was despondent about the state of the world and felt that she couldn't live with having so much while others had so little.

After walking all night in the woods, she decided she would dedicate her life to peace. In 1952, she became the first woman to hike the Appalachian Trail in one season. In 1953, she renamed herself Peace Pilgrim and began what became a 25,000-mile pilgrimage across America. She took a vow of poverty, committing to live through the generosity of others and never accept more than she needed.

Each day, she walked until she was offered shelter. Each night before she went to sleep, she passed on anything given to her that she hadn't used. She woke each morning with nothing but the clothes she wore and the things she could carry in her pockets: a comb, a pen and her current writing.

In *Peace Pilgrim: Her Life and Work in Her Own Words*, a compilation of her writings over those years, she said, "So I got busy on a very interesting project. This was to live all the good things I believed in. I did not confuse myself by trying to take them all at once, but rather if I was doing something that I knew I shouldn't be doing, I stopped doing it."

Peace Pilgrim walked until her death in 1981, when she was killed instantly in a car crash while being driven to a speaking engagement. She inspired countless people. Today, hundreds of volunteers continue to translate her teachings into different languages to distribute them freely around the world.

Why am I telling you all this? Because this story is just one of many examples that prove we don't have to live lives we hate.

We can decide to do jobs we don't love for a while to put together some money—I did it. George Clooney did it.

We can work at jobs we don't love that allow us time and energy to play and create in the ways we want to.

We can take a vow of poverty and sleep on other peoples' couches for a while.

And whatever we choose to do, change will come.

Humans evolve—that's what it means to be human. Wherever you are, there is always a way out of situations that dim your lights.

Your Yes Statement

On a new page of your notebook, write everything you know right now about what you want to accomplish in your life, everything you want to give back to the world. As much as you can right now, describe your light.

What do you offer your friends and family?

What are things you can do, now or within a few years of preparation, that would pay for the kind of life you want to live?

What are the things you can see yourself contributing to the world, now and in the future?

Here is my yes statement:

I, Gezim Gashi, will positively change the lives of young people by preparing them to shape the entertainment industry, making entertainment culture a force of inspiration, connection and love.

I will serve my family, friends and community as a source of support, inspiration and positive energy.

Now you:

I, ... **, will** ....

....

....

by ....

....

I will serve ....

....

Chapter 5

The Power of a Dream

Having a dream is being in relationship with yourself and your mission.

Once you know who you are, you'll know what makes you happy and what you can contribute to the world. The intersection of those two factors is your dream, a vision that no one else in the world can share.

As I write this, we're still at the height of the COVID-19 pandemic, and so much of the world is on hold. So many wonderful books have been published that wait on store shelves; so many concerts have been cancelled. Businesses have failed.

For so many people with a dream, this last year has been a nightmare. But the amazing thing about having a dream is that it keeps us moving forward and developing new strengths—it is something that inspires us onward even more than it is something we achieve. A clear vision is a light that draws us forward, keeping us on the path toward success as we define it.

Our commitment to our dream is a decision that informs all other decisions.

The power of a dream is in its clarity. That doesn't mean it won't change—it absolutely will. But it must be powered by passion, by emotions that will realign us and our decisions even after something like a pandemic.

There are many ways you can add power to your dream.

Symbols have been important throughout history because they are effective at bringing the power of huge concepts into small spaces. If your dream is to help people reach the heights of the entertainment business, as mine is, a photo of a Grammy award can be a regular reminder of why you're making that call when you really don't feel like making that call.

In *The Path of Least Resistance: Learning to Become the Creative Force in Your Own Life,* author Robert Fritz wrote about the importance of dreaming our own dreams: "If you limit your choices to what seems possible or reasonable, you disconnect yourself from what you truly want, and all that's left is a compromise."

Compromise is not a superpower.

Fritz went on to share his framework for becoming a creative force:

Current Reality

Where are you today in relation to where you want to be?

Action Steps

What do you need to do to move from your current reality to your realized vision? Start with the largest steps (I need a college degree and seed money) and break them down into manageable chunks of action.

The Path of Least Resistance

Your Vision

Remember, the more detail, color and texture, the more power your vision has. Find images, write about it, tell friends about it ... do everything you can to make it real.

So, before we go any further, it's time to describe your dream. Maybe that's easy—perhaps you've been carrying it around for a while, and you just need to do a little update.

Or maybe you've been trying to figure out what to do with your life for years without getting any closer to a vision. No problem. Let's do it together.

First, describe your ideal workday.

- What are you doing?
- Where are you doing it?
- Who are you doing it with?
- How do you feel?

Awesome. Now, describe your ideal playday.

- What are you doing?
- Where are you doing it?
- Who are you doing it with?
- How do you feel?

"Wait!" you might be thinking. "I want to spend my days [say,] painting and making art. Who is going to pay me for that right now?

"I need to pay my bills."

Such an excellent point.

But do not worry about that right now—do everything you can to not think about it at all. In fact, it can be helpful to think about what we enjoyed doing when we were children because we hadn't yet closed the door on a lot of opportunities we were told weren't practical.

Think about it: someone helps Beyoncé get dressed for her concerts. Someone got to be Prince's drummer. There is someone in the world right now whose job is to play with Kate and William's adorable kids. Yet if you told your parents that one of these things is what you planned to do with your life, they'd probably be mortified.

To plan your best life, your greatest contribution to the world, cast off the limitations you feel the world has placed upon you—at least for the length of time it takes to do this exercise.

If you want to spend your days making art, your challenge right now might be to figure out how to pay your bills while leaving as much time and energy as possible for your creative work. It makes sense that the more effectively you do that, the better you'll become at your art, and the more time you'll have to make essential connections. What you don't want to do is sell yourself short and decide that art isn't something you're meant to do.

Once we know what we love doing and are great at, we will start to find new ways to make it happen. Windows will open for us, and we'll be ready to leap through them.

A friend of mine who teaches women to be welders and pipefitters told me the story of a student who loved horses and wanted to spend her life with them.

First, she trained as a veterinary assistant and got her dream job in a practice that mainly treated horses. It wasn't long, though, before she realized she was spending her time with horses in the worst moments of their lives, and she was earning not much more than minimum wage. It was terrible.

After sinking into a depression for a few months, she realized that her pain was telling her something important. She had to quit her job.

She moved back home, and after getting clearer on her dream, she trained as a tradesperson, a pipefitter. Now she works six months of the year in the North in camps and has six months a year off to spend with her horses on her ranch. The ranch that she was able to buy after just a few years of working as a pipefitter!

Each year, as she pays off her mortgage and puts money away in savings, she reduces the amount of time she spends away. She'll be retiring decades early to raise horses.

In other words, your path doesn't have to be straight. It doesn't have to look like anything anyone has ever done before.

I mentioned George Clooney. Before he became an actor, he tried out for the Cincinnati Reds baseball team. He didn't make it. Then he sold shoes. Then he sold insurance.

Jon Hamm of Mad Men was a high school drama teacher.

Those jobs weren't missteps—they were *steps*.

Whatever you're doing right now, you're going to enjoy it a lot more and bring more passion to it if you remember that this *is* your path.

Your Vision Map

To make it easier to keep that in mind, let's create your vision map. We've already addressed some of these questions, and some we'll address in greater depth later in the book. For now, you're just trying to sketch out a detailed vision of the life you're aiming to build, that life that will allow you to use all of your superpowers.

WHO?
Who are the people in your professional life? In your personal life? What are their qualities, passions and values?

WHAT?
What do you do on your workdays? What do you do on your playdays? How much overlap is there?

WHERE?
Describe the environments that you work and play in. City? Country? Small town? Manhattan? In the mountains? Loft? Shared office space? Stage?

WHEN?
Break down your workdays and playdays, hour by hour. What time do you wake up and go to sleep? What hours do you work? When will you spend time with friends? When will you reflect on your life?

WHY?

Finding your why is the entirety of Chapter 10, but for now, just write what comes to mind for you. In your dream life, why do you do what you do? Think of it as a primer for the thinking you'll do between now and then.

Your Current Reality

Go through the same exercise, answering all the same questions about your life today.

What's the who, what, where, when and why of your days right now?

The more you know about your current reality, the more likely it is you'll be able to map your way to your vision. (Columbus didn't know much about the world and ended up in America thinking it was India. Don't be Columbus.)

Being honest with yourself about the gap between where you are right now and where you want to be will allow you to map your action steps. Mapping your action steps will ensure that your energy and resources move you up the right ladder.

Your Action Steps

You won't be able to identify all the steps you need to take to move you from where you are today to the life you've envisioned for yourself, but you will see some of them. Write them down and begin breaking them into smaller steps. Google "SMART goals"—and then translate each of your action steps into a series of SMART goals.

The Power of Commitment

In December of 2017, I was invited to interview with a global media company at their office in New York.

It was a surreal winter day. I took an iconic yellow cab to their offices overlooking the Empire State Building, and the snow was coming down in huge flakes.

The people I spoke to at the company were interested in working with me. But they told me that I'd have to launch my own company for it to work with their business model.

The meeting was life-changing. After I left, I stood in the street outside the building with the snow falling on me. I realized I'd reached the next level—it was time to leave my comfort zone and my employment contracts. When I landed in Paris, I called my brother, who has always been hugely supportive of me, and told him that I wanted to start a company. I'd call it, "By Gezim Gashi," BGG, which included his initials, BG.

I had become clear on what I wanted to do, how I wanted to do it and the kind of people I wanted to do it with. Forming my own organization made that possible.

It meant that I had to leave the students I was working with in Sweden, which was very difficult. My position there was unique—I was not a teacher but a mentor, and I knew that there wouldn't be anyone else to fill that role. It would be a loss to them.

After I left, I quickly understood that we could still be in touch—I could still mentor them—but at the time, it was hard.

On my way home, I called Jim and Mary Kay. We'd been talking about launching an institute together.

"I know we can do something no one has ever done," I said. "We're the right team."

So often, we hear about people doing exciting things and think, "Oh, I wish I could do that."

You can do that.

We are swimming in good ideas. You hear about the ones you do because those people *acted* on their ideas. They made the decision. They committed to the losses, the risks and the work.

Ideas need that moment of commitment. We need that moment of commitment.

For me, it happened near the Empire State Building in the snow, but it could have been anywhere. We just need that moment of realization, when we ask ourselves if we are meant to do more than what we're doing.

I knew that was true for me.

I was loyal to my students and our team in Sweden, so I felt pulled in two directions. Yet once I made that commitment, I realized that I could open even more doors for my students—because I'd taken those steps forward myself.

One of my friends uses the metaphor of windows. She says that mentors and other inspiring people open windows for us; the way we land when we leap through those windows is entirely up to us.

That's what happened to me in that meeting—a new window of opportunity was opened. But it was after the meeting, standing on the street, that I leapt through that window and committed to making the most of that new freedom.

Once I did, everything started to happen for me. The words usually attributed to the great eighteenth-century writer Johann Wolfgang von Goethe have almost become a cliché, but they became true in my life: "Boldness has genius, power and magic in it."

Chapter 6

The Power of Play & Passion

Psychiatrist Dr. Stuart Brown was working with a group of young men in Texas when he realized that, in addition to being convicted murderers, they all had something else in common: an almost complete absence of play in their childhoods.

This realization led him to study the connections between play and success, and his TED talk on the subject has been watched more than two million times. His research, along with many other studies, has proven that we need play, just as we need sleep, to be fully healthy and productive.

Play makes us feel alive. It eases our worries and renews our natural sense of optimism.

Play is a critical element in building community; playing with others builds bonds of trust, says Dr. Brown. At both the individual and community level, human beings are "built to play and built through play."

Play and passion ignite us, refueling our energy. They keep us going long after willpower and self-discipline have deserted us.

You may have been taught that play is frivolous. But whether we do it for money or to replenish ourselves during our time off, doing what we love is *essential* to our health, happiness, creativity, relationships—and to the world we live in.

It's *How* You Do What You Love

In 1986, Marsha Sinetar published *Do What You Love, the Money Will Follow: Discovering Your Right Livelihood*. It became a huge bestseller. The problem, though, was that many readers launched businesses making gift baskets or started a wedding band, and the money did not follow.

Regrettably, they'd taken a narrow view of the concept.

If you do what you love, the money will follow, but you won't necessarily make a living by being paid to do the thing that you love doing.

This is true of literally millions of poets, dancers, musicians, visual artists and theatre actors—of the many who begin, only a tiny fraction ends up making anything like a middle-class living through their arts.

But millions more have creative, happy and fulfilling lives by using whatever it is they love to fuel their energy and build their communities. Following their joy leads them to rewarding work and supportive, nourishing communities.

This truth has been a powerful theme in my own life. Earlier in the book, I mentioned Musikhuset, the afterschool music café in Växjö. It was led by Micke Ringdahl, who told us about the successful Swedish songwriter and producer Andreas Carlsson. Born in Tingsryd, forty minutes from Alvesta where I'm from, Andreas has sold more than 150 million albums and been nominated for six Grammys and two Emmys. He's worked with Celine Dion, the Backstreet Boys and NSYNC.

At that time, when I was fourteen and fifteen, the biggest songs in the world were his.

I loved singing and writing music, and so I'd take the bus to Musikhuset every Wednesday. We could record and meet other people our age who were interested in music, which was mind-blowing because there was no social media then. It was very unusual to be able to connect with people with shared passions when you were from a small town.

One day, Micke Ringdahl took us to another music organization in Tingsryd called Kulturverkstan, which Andreas had financed and built. We were out of our minds with excitement. We couldn't believe it. Magnus Lundin, the principal, talked about Andreas's success, this massive star who had come from the same quiet part of Sweden as us. And I remember I was just, like, "I can't believe that someone like Andreas has been in this room." We sat in the chair where he had sat and thought, "This is insane!"

Those Wednesday evenings were pure play.

I started to do a lot of YouTube videos, and Andreas became a Swedish Idol judge with two of his friends; their show was super popular. Along with the Idol show, they had a program called "Made in Sweden." Through it, they wanted to find ten people they believed would do great things in the entertainment industry.

They chose me to be one of them. I was nineteen, and it was the first time I had seen Stockholm. It was a big deal for me.

We went into a studio, and Andreas talked about doing "Waking Up in Vegas" with Katy Perry, which was a huge hit at that time, and sang and played for us. I introduced myself and told him that I had met with Magnus, Andreas's early mentor and music teacher. And I told him how inspired I'd been by him and his work after finding out that he was from our part of Sweden—how much it meant to me to learn that you didn't have to be from LA or New York to be successful in the entertainment industry.

After that, we stayed in touch.

In 2014, I was getting millions of hits on YouTube, and I had returned to LA to study business at a college in Santa Monica. Magnus and I were both nominated for an award in Sweden, and I returned home for the ceremony. Magnus won the award for his work with Andreas at the music school they'd opened. I reintroduced myself and reminded Magnus that we'd met when I was fourteen, almost exactly ten years before. I told him how that experience had changed my life.

Playing Together

Magnus asked me to come and meet with him and Andreas before I went back to LA. The plan was to meet for a thirty-minute lunch; we ended up spending six hours together. Finally, Andreas said, "You should be the head of marketing of our school."

I went home and told my family I was moving back. I wasn't going back to LA.

At fourteen, I wanted to sing and write music. I had no aspirations to be an educator or work with students or launch a music school. But I knew enough to seek out other people who loved what I loved, who shared my passion for changing the world through music. And that was enough—play and passion led me to the opportunities that turned out to be so much more important to me.

I learned that my true calling is helping other people find and build their dreams through music and entertainment. Through story, play and passion.

Finding Your Playmates

Now that you know how important play can be, I'd like you to go back to your notebook and make a list of everything that feels like play to you.

List anything that comes to mind, from shopping with a friend to trying a new recipe to choreographing a new dance routine to reading a good book.

Once you feel your list is complete, make a new list: what are some ways to connect with other people who share these definitions of play?

Social media is an obvious one, of course, but do not underestimate the power of person-to-person contact. As soon as you can, try to turn online contacts into real-life connections in play situations.

Asking someone for coffee is asking them for a precious gift—their time. But asking them to experience your shared passion together is *fire*, especially if those passions aren't wildly popular.

Play × Vulnerability = Magic

Not long after I started working at the school in Tingsryd, I met Jim and Mary Kay, with whom I would eventually launch the institute in LA.

I was doing so well at the school, and the people there loved the passion and ideas I was bringing to our work.

Then a tragedy happened: my cousin in Kosovo died suddenly, leaving two small children, devastating our family. I was devastated.

My mom and I went back to Kosovo, and, of course, I thought about my last one-on-one conversation with my cousin.

He'd said, "I really wish I lived in a place where my children could get the best education."

At the time we spoke, I wasn't yet working in education. The fact that I was now employed at a school, working to give young people the best education, somehow felt like both a blessing and a message.

When I got back to work, I was told that some people were coming from Los Angeles because they'd heard about what we were doing and wanted to see it for themselves. I immediately felt that they would be important in my life, which proved to be so true.

I arranged for some of the students to sing; one performed a new song they'd written. I was standing off to the side, and I could tell that Jim and Mary Kay were enjoying it. At some point, Andreas brought them over to meet me, and there was an instant click, a recognition that we could do amazing things together.

Mary Kay and I had a chance to talk, and for some reason, I felt I had to tell her about what had happened with my cousin and how he had inspired me to create something entirely new in education. We had a completely honest, open conversation, and she was so empathetic.

We found we believed in a lot of the same things and started to spend a lot of time together—Jim and Mary Kay became like family to me.

When you share passion, play together, and are vulnerable in your conversations, you get to know each other in a way that isn't otherwise possible. You build bonds of trust, and you want to do more together because it makes you feel more alive.

You know that, together, you can take risks that wouldn't be possible alone, because you each bring your best to the process.

We realized almost instantly that we were all committed to having an impact on young people through our work and that we had a similar mission to change music education. The industry had changed so much that traditional approaches just weren't effective anymore, and we began working together on new global platforms to prepare students for the future.

Our work together just grew from there.

In 2017, just after a terrible terrorist event in Sweden, when five people were killed by a truck driven into a crowd, our Swedish students and ten students from Los Angeles performed a sold-out concert at the U.S. embassy in Stockholm. Then we brought ten of our Swedish students to LA to perform there. It was such a healing, spectacular series, and none of it would have happened without the connections and teamwork sparked in that initial meeting with Mary Kay and Jim.

If I'd walked up to Magnus and asked him to introduce me to Andreas, or I'd met Andreas and asked him to hire me at his school, or I'd been employed at the school and asked Mary Kay and Jim if they wanted to build new global institutes for music students, it's highly improbable that their answers would have been, "Sure, Gezim, let's do that."

But because we built bonds through our shared passions, play and vulnerability, those connections happened naturally and organically.

Whatever you do to pay your bills, playing with others in the ways you're passionate about will create a space for wonderful things to happen in your life.

And like me, you may eventually find that your dreams— in my case, at age fourteen, to have a huge hit song—are way too small.

Through your connections with others, you'll find that your impact on the world is meant to be much more significant than just changing your own life.

Chapter 7

The Power of Authentic Presence and Connection

Authenticity is the superpower that enables all other superpowers.

What do I mean by authenticity? It's a word that's overused a lot right now, so it's worth examining what we're aiming for when we talk about it.

The classic dictionary definition is just being genuine, but this confuses a lot of people. It doesn't mean that we act on every emotion that flashes through us. It doesn't mean that we say every word that goes through our minds.

In my experience, being authentic is a two-part effort. First, we must be true to our best selves. Then we must show up as our best selves in our interactions whenever possible.

Does that mean we never make mistakes, never stumble in our interactions with others? Absolutely not. We will make mistakes. We will do and say things we later regret or just realize were ineffective at getting us closer to what we hoped to achieve. Authenticity in this scenario is being able to say, "Wow, I messed up there. I'm sorry, and I hope you'll give me another chance to do better." It's remembering that we learn more from our stumbles than we do from our triumphs. If we aren't stumbling regularly, we aren't moving fast enough. Mistakes are an inevitable, essential part of our developmental evolution.

One synonym for authenticity might be vulnerability, the way social researcher Brené Brown uses that word. She has popularized the idea of vulnerability as something to which we should constantly aspire.

Here is how she describes it in a conversation with a journalist, which she recounts in the introduction to her brilliant book, *Rising Strong*. The journalist approached her and said he wanted to work on his issues around vulnerability, courage and authenticity, and asked her to spell out the upside and downside.

She tells him that she believes that "vulnerability—the willingness to show up and be seen with no guarantee of outcome—is the only path to more love, belonging and joy." The downside, she says, is that doing the work meant that he would "stumble, fall and get his ass kicked."

She goes on to say that this work is the work of living a wholehearted life.

Later in the book, in the chapter "The Physics of Vulnerability," she says: "If we are brave enough often enough, we will fall. This is the physics of vulnerability."

Let's think about what we know about authentic, vulnerable connection, then.

1. We must know ourselves well enough that we are not showing up with the intent of seeing who we are in other peoples' eyes.

Only then can we see them instead of our own reflection.

And only when we see them can we connect with them.

2. We must know how to still our mind to the degree that we can be truly present.

If our mind is running its game somewhere else, focused on yesterday or tomorrow or that other deal over there, we cannot connect because we are not *there*.

3. We must be honest about who we are and what is going on with us—no masks, no filters, no agendas.

When we look at someone through masks, ours or theirs, their agenda or our own, we are distant from each other even when sitting across a table.

It's only when the masks come off and we put our agendas aside that connection can happen.

Women are often socialized to be better at this. They are taught that trust is essential to collaboration, and that we can only trust people who share themselves and their lives with us. The masculine model, the patriarchal model, is the one in which people trust each other based on who they know—your grandfather knew my grandfather, so I know you're a good guy. Or, if you're not, your family will make good on any promises you make.

For many reasons, that patriarchal world is less and less valid. Sure, it exists in some small but important pockets. But because of social media, it is less influential than ever before.

The most influential and effective world leaders during the pandemic were women. But people of all genders can be authentic leaders when they show up as their whole selves and allow themselves to feel and lead with empathy.

Social Media, Globalism and Authenticity

We have just emerged from a time when being "professional" meant we left our authentic selves at home. At work, we put on a series of masks and applied strategies of persuasion and influence through filters and Photoshop, literal or metaphoric.

The personal was personal.

That world is dying, along with traditional advertising.

Knowing and being honest about who we are—showing up as our whole selves—is increasingly understood to be the only effective way to connect with our people *and* our market, whatever field we're in. In fact, more and more, the term "market" doesn't mean anything at all. Our people are the community that nourishes us, and it is the community we are meant to nourish.

I didn't always know this. But in 2013, I met Quincy Jones III at an event in Los Angeles. Steve Angello was then one of the biggest house DJs in the world, and he was receiving an award from the Swedish-American Chamber of Commerce.

Waiting for the ceremony to begin, I started talking to the person sitting next to me and was impressed by how kind he seemed. I told him about some of the difficulties of trying to succeed in entertainment as a refugee in Sweden, and he understood. He told me that his mom is Swedish, and he said he'd also struggled when he moved there at sixteen because, like me, he didn't look Swedish.

We reconnected later at a party in the Hollywood Hills and started a conversation that has continued on and off since then.

As we talked about making things happen in the music industry in the U.S., I said, "It's all about who you know."

His reply would change my life.

"No. It's not about who you know," he said. "It's about *how* you know them."

Until I learned this truth, I believed that a certain kind of person was successful, and if we weren't like those people, we should try to act like them.

After growing up in a small town in Sweden, when I was in the U.S. with the accomplished people I wanted to work with, people with fame and success, it was almost like I was with aliens. It wasn't that I wasn't myself, but I was always thinking about how I should behave.

The idea of "it's who you know" shuttered my light. When I met successful people, it wasn't so much that I was superficial but that I was locked in a dream in which they were different than me, that they were somehow born to success, and I was not. I complimented their work and asked for a business card. Whatever we talked about, the subtext of the conversation was about what I wanted—without meaning to be, I was a bit selfish because I thought my goal in that moment was supposed to be to impress them.

When Quincy said, "It's about *how* you know them," it changed everything for me because it allowed me to be myself.

When I meet people now, I am just me, and we connect naturally. We talk about things that are happening in our lives.

Yesterday I had a conversation with a radio personality about this. We talked about that feeling you have when a person isn't really with you, when they're trying to impress you or convince you of something.

Humans can feel it when we've connected authentically, and we can feel it when we haven't. Being entirely myself means that I attract people I'm aligned with, and I don't attract people I'm not aligned with.

Business relationships don't have to be transactional. They don't have to be about wanting to spend time with successful people; connection is never about trying to impress other people with your qualities or your accomplishments.

When you make genuine connections with like-minded people, those connections often develop into honest, authentic relationships, and magic can happen. You may have opportunities to work together or become friends who have conversations that change your way of seeing yourself or the world. They will want you to succeed, just as you will want them to succeed. Helping each other will bring you both happiness.

Many people think that they need successful people because those people are the ladder to their own success. I now know that's wrong. You never have more value as a person because you've had a meeting with someone else and received recognition from them.

But when we have authentic conversations, real things can happen. When we talk about what's real and important for us, our dreams may align.

If we think it's about "who you know," we are followers. When we understand it's about "how you know them," we are all leaders.

When you don't understand this, it's easy to believe it's all about asking for favors. Today, people think that they can reach out and ask me to help them just because they have my contact information. But when I meet with people, we usually don't even talk about the reasons for our meeting—I might notice a golf photo of them in their office, so we talk about that. It's not about me pretending I like golf, but about following the clues they offer to really get to know them as a person.

If I'm not authentic, it isn't fun. And if it isn't fun, you're not inspiring other people to be themselves with you.

When I meet with people, it is because we enjoy being together. I bring my excitement because I want the meeting to create something for both of us. I want them to also be inspired and motivated.

It doesn't always happen, but when you have this mentality, it doesn't matter. When you go to a meeting and you've been fully yourself, you'll make a human connection 99 percent of the time. The timing might be wrong for shared projects or even a social relationship, but we can still talk and follow each other on social media. And it's fascinating how often those connections will later turn into alignments.

Until I learned this from Quincy, my business conversations were about business. If the business proposal didn't work out, we both left the meeting with nothing.

Using my friend's analogy, let's say we have a window of opportunity.

In the old mindset, when I jumped, I looked for a safe landing.

With the new, authentic mindset, I'll look for the landing that aligns with my strengths—and because I've developed genuine relationships, my community is there for me as I jump. And that makes all the difference.

We're not lucky because we meet famous or succesful people—we're lucky when we meet inspiring people. Someone who lives around the corner might say something that changes your life.

Dropping the idea that fame, success and money determine our value—and that celebrities arc of greater value than others—will make us a lot happier. It will also allow us to be more inspired by life.

I went to the U.S. because I felt I had to meet those celebrities to succeed. To "expand my network." But I found that many of them were depressed and doing lots of very bad stuff. That's not a life that anyone wants.

When Quincy taught me that it's about how you know people, he also taught me that real success is about the impact you have on other people.

Now I am fortunate enough to travel around the world and spend time in amazing places with amazing people. On social media, people see that as happiness. I am happy—but only because I can meet people and be there for them, to help them do the great stuff they want to do. It has nothing to do with being invited to the right parties.

My conversation with Quincy in the Hollywood Hills inspired me to be authentic, to be myself in everything I did. And it also made me understand that success and happiness are all about *why* you're doing what you're doing.

Authentic Service

I grew up in an incredibly unique environment, one in which my parents taught me that I am special and can do anything I put my mind to doing. When I work with students, however, I'm reminded that many people grow up without ever hearing this kind of affirmative support.

This is one of the ways I serve the people I work with: I become the mirror that reflects their potential back to them. By pushing them to reach higher and think bigger—to start to believe in themselves by proving they can reach their goals—I'm able to pass on the gifts my parents gave to me.

I'm always on the lookout for the talents of others, and I can help them move toward their dreams simply by multiplying their passion with my own. That is the way authentic connection works—it does not add our respective talents but multiplies them. As I experience success in helping my students, I am more empowered in everything I do.

Really, if you are feeling stuck today, not sure how to move forward, there is nothing more powerful that I can offer you than this advice: Go find someone to help. Throw all your skills, talents, experience and passion at helping them rise, with no expectation of return or even thanks. Do it to unleash the energy that is currently stagnant in you.

Now, celebrate their success. You will find that magical things start to happen for you too.

Being Present

As I wrote earlier, when you're thinking about yourself, you're not truly present for other people.

When you're not present, it is impossible to make a truly authentic connection. You're not there. You're in your head—thinking about what they think about you and whether you're saying the right thing, whether that look on their face means they're interested in working with you or they're just looking forward to their lunch.

This is the state in which many of us move through the world.

When you are truly present to another person, you will both remember that meeting, sometimes forever. You will think about them; they will think about you. When we talk about the superpower of authenticity, we're also talking about true presence because you cannot be authentic without being present.

The reason that true presence is so rare is that it requires **a lot** of work to get to that place.

It requires knowing who you are to the degree that you are not looking to other people to give you signals about who they think you are.

It requires knowing your value to the world so that you don't wander around looking for other people's opinions on your value.

It requires knowing what you're here to contribute to others.

Trying to impress people is the opposite of being present for them. Everything else in this book, to some degree, is about making sure that you'll never feel that need.

Chapter 8
The Power of Resilience

I feel like this would be an entirely different chapter if I weren't writing it during a pandemic when we have all learned a lot about our individual resilience, but here goes.

In *Resilience: Hard-Won Wisdom for Living a Better Life*, former Navy Seal Eric Greitens writes, "Resilience is the virtue that enables people to move through hardship and become better. No one escapes pain, fear and suffering. Yet from pain can come wisdom, from fear can come courage, from suffering can come strength—if we have the virtue of resilience."

In my experience, this final phrase is so important. Not everyone learns from their mistakes. Not everyone becomes stronger because of their suffering. The sad truth is that many of us will go through life making the same mistakes over and over again, never moving forward.

Many of us won't learn nearly as much as we could because we lock our understanding of the world into our self-image and reject anything that doesn't fit our current view.

And many of us will turn suffering into bitterness and neurosis rather than compassion and strength.

What distinguishes those who rise from those who stay down? Resilience.

The Power of "I Don't Know"

Before I go on, I want to be clear that I'm not providing an excuse to judge or shame other people. We don't know, we never know, what other people have suffered. We don't know where they are in their journey or what they have survived to get to where they are, no matter how humble that place is.

When we compare ourselves to others, judging the place we see them in today, we may be comparing the equivalent of our performance in kindergarten gym class to their Olympic finals. We don't know.

It may sound like I'm off on a tangent, but this is a critically important resilience tool. Whenever we are judging other people, we are strengthening a mindset that shames us too. And shame is a toxin. It drains our energy, our passion, our self-confidence and our compassion. Shaming ourselves or others is like drinking poison.

So, when you find yourself judging others, make this your mantra: "I don't know."

You know almost nothing about that person or their journey. This is true of your neighbors, and it may even be true of people in your family, because so many of our battles are internal.

Now, just in case you are shaming yourself right now for being a Judgy McJudgerson, let me remind you that this instinct is hardwired in us. It kept us safer on the African savannah when we were emerging as a species, and regrettably, it has not evolved out of us because being a well-behaved part of a tribe still keeps us safer. (Not happier, just safer.) It is as natural as having a sweet tooth or scratching an itch. Forgive yourself. (It will help you learn to forgive others, too.)

But in the twenty-first century, it is an instinct that destroys our ability to connect with others and to be our best selves. So here is your shaming antidote: "I don't know."

Okay, back to the other elements of resilience.

Resilience and Reality

There are few things more disabling than the belief that we are supposed to feel good and that things are supposed to go well in our lives all the time. If we have these beliefs, it is natural to self-shame when we don't feel good and to be devastated when bad things happen.

A woman I know lost her husband to early-onset Alzheimer's disease. When I asked her how she had coped in the early years after his diagnosis and said how hard it must have been, she said, "Who am I to think that I should get through life unscathed?

"We all experience tragedy. We had such a great life together. This is our tragedy. This is our experience of that part of life."

Who knows what it cost her to come to this incredible strength and philosophical outlook? What I do know is that doing so allows her to live a joyous, loving, active life despite more than a decade of visiting a man she loves who hasn't recognized her once in all of those years.

In her book *When Things Fall Apart,* the revered Buddhist teacher Pema Chödrön writes that our acceptance of hopelessness and death is the beginning of our real lives. It is only when we understand that "there is no solid ground to stand on" that we can start to live fully, she teaches. Only when we understand that we will not be spared—but that we will find the strength to bear the suffering—can we love and live fully.

In so many ways, resilience is acceptance. It is the ability to shake off the feeling that bad things should not happen to us, to accept that of course they will, and to move through the bad times with as much grace as we can manage.

When that grace isn't within reach, it is the ability to accept that too.

Resilience and Self-Care

The pandemic sped up a trend that had been emerging over the last decade, a movement away from the idea of the human body as a machine and toward the concept of nurturing ourselves like gardens.

What a revolutionary shift! We are starting to understand that we can't be our best in our work if we don't also have healthy relationships and time to eat right, play and be active.

Another trend is the acceptance of mental health care as a wellness issue. The pandemic has taught us that we are all vulnerable to brain and mood disorders such as depression and anxiety. We've all learned that our risks increase in situations where our lives are out of balance and we don't have time for preventative wellness or to manage stress.

In his book *Emotional First Aid,* psychologist Guy Winch talks about the importance of healing from emotional wounds in the same way we work to recover from physical injuries. With trauma and loss, he recommends a two-step way to find meaning in the experience: first asking ourselves why something happened and then finding something positive that has come out of our suffering. This isn't toxic positivity, which asks us to hide our pain and slap a smile on it, but a deep dive into the meaning of life and death, and a way to reclaim our power in the face of random tragedy.

We can't stop bad things from happening, and we can't control the way they unfold—but we can work to ensure that we turn them into something meaningful in our lives.

Winch also talks about the importance of relieving guilt by apologizing effectively, changing our behavior and forgiving ourselves. If we don't do this, we carry around an idea of ourselves as bad, as someone who has let others down. This is what it means to be human, to try and sometimes fail; freeing ourselves from the burden of guilt also frees us to be our best. No one was ever shamed into being a stronger person, and that most certainly includes us.

He defines an effective apology as one that contains four elements:

- saying we're sorry,
- validating the other person's feelings about our actions and expressing remorse,
- making things right through some kind of compensation, and
- then promising not to do the same things again.

To forgive ourselves, he offers an equally straightforward process: take responsibility for what we did and how it affected others, make sure we never do it again, and find a way to make amends through some kind of action. By doing this, he writes, we can forgive ourselves and move forward.

When We Fail

There is no way to fail in our culture without it taking a toll on our self-esteem. It takes a lot of practice to fail without feeling shame and questioning our worth.

The key to making this work is to have a failure recovery strategy in place. In the chapter on creative collaborations, I write about a study that found that people with supportive partners were more likely to take risks. Although the study didn't go into the cause of this phenomenon, it's a safe bet to assume that it is because being surrounded by people who believe in us makes failure much easier to recover from.

In *Emotional First Aid,* Winch talks about the importance of spending time with people who care about us whenever we're healing from an emotional wound. And while this is always true, it is probably hardest to put into action when we fail. For this reason, before we go any further, I'd like you to think about the person in your life who you can trust to be there for you in this way. Talk to them today and let them know that you're committing to being completely honest with them the next time you feel you've failed. Ask them to do the same with you. Just knowing you have this support system in place will make it easier for you to reach higher and step outside of your comfort zone more often.

Remember too that this entire book is a series of steps making it possible to claim your superpowers. You won't need to do this once, but many times. Don't lose track of your copy—whenever you fail, lose sight of your best self or just lose your mojo, walk through these steps again, this time with the new knowledge you've gained since the last time. You'll always find new strength and clarity in the process.

Finding the Treasures in Tragedy

When my cousin died suddenly in Kosovo, our family was heartbroken. It was so hard. Yet we gathered and found strength in our love for each other and our memories of him. It was a terrible time in our lives, and I knew that my life would never be the same.

What I didn't imagine was that it would be better.

Despite the terrible loss we still feel, my last conversation with my cousin deepened my commitment to education. Everything I do now is strengthened by his presence in my heart and memory. When my energy starts to lessen, I return to that moment with him, and I find I can go on.

I built a cinema in my home so that I can entertain my nieces and nephews. I wanted to give them a space to hang out and just be there for each other. And I wanted to spend time with them and do what I can to make sure that they feel excited about the future.

When I reach for resilience, I think of their smiles and laughter.

When we accept the tragedies that are part of the lives we're blessed with, we also find treasures in those experiences. Resilience is the ability to go through hard times *and* the ability to transform those lessons into building blocks for the next steps in our life.

The Power of Seasons

One of my favorite memes shows up again every autumn: "The leaves are about to teach us the beauty of letting go."

We have so much to learn from the natural world. The glorious energy of spring, when tiny green things reappear from the earth and shoot for the sky; the joyous relaxations of summer; the harvest of the fall and the dormancy of winter. The seasons teach us that there is a time for everything.

I've found there is so much power in holding these lessons close in tough times.

When I realized I'd chosen the wrong school for me in Los Angeles, it would have been so easy to push forward and try to make the best of it. But I somehow knew that it was not the time to push through, but to retreat.

I thought I'd be in entertainment school meeting Hollywood stars; instead, I found myself working to save more money in a job I did not love. It was a time of saving, of waiting for new information and inspiration.

As I worked, that inspiration bubbled up to the surface, and I began making YouTube videos and growing my channel.

That growth energy was there, but for a while, it was underground. I could have become despondent. I might have even given up.

Instead, because I knew my story, I knew that I was simply in a season, one that would transform into something else if I just stayed true to myself.

Knowing that was a source of strength, a source of resilience. It meant that, when new opportunities came my way, I was as passionate and positive as I'd ever been. I was ready.

Chapter 9

The Power of Creative Collaboration

After the student concerts that we produced in Sweden and then Los Angeles, there came a moment when I knew that it was time for me to leave Sweden.

We were all sitting together having dinner before our trip back home the next day, and I realized it was time to create something entirely new, an entertainment school for high school students in the heart of the entertainment industry, LA.

When I met Jim and Mary Kay, I was twenty-four. I hadn't really done much, but they believed in my potential—they believed in the things I wanted to do. When I met them, they had so many reasons to say something like, "Get back to us when you have more knowledge, more tools, more success." But they believed in what I was going to do.

From the very beginning, our relationship felt like loyalty for life. They opened their home to me when I came to the

United States, and when I'm in the U.S., there is never a question about where I'll spend Thanksgiving.

By the time I met them, I understood who I wanted to be, and it was that future Gezim they believed in.

Sometimes people decide who they want to work with based on other peoples' successes, as if life is a ladder and people higher on the ladder are there to help you climb.

As we explored earlier, that's a mistake.

Your team needs to be made up of people who believe in you, who inspire you.

Once you determine who you want to be in the world, your most important goal should be surrounding yourself with people who inspire you to be that person, only more so. You can always find people with the right skill sets to complete a project, but it is just as important to find people who bring out the best in you and in whom you bring out the best.

If you have followed each of the action steps in the book so far, you're now ready to activate your next superpower—creating the right team.

Finding Your Who

In the Story of You exercise we did in Chapter 2, you learned how to describe the hero of your story, your best self.

Now I'd like you to go back to that chapter and use the same exercises to identify the characteristics of the people you'd like to make up your community.

What values, passions, talents and neuroses do you share? What skills, experience and attributes might they contribute to co-projects to fill gaps in your own contributions?

Describe their "energy," their personality and their passions. What do they bring that you don't? What do you like about the way they manage conflict? What do you want to learn from them? What have they done to prove that you can trust them with your vulnerability?

In new pages in your notebook, describe the qualities and characteristics of people you imagine in the following roles.

1. YOUR DREAM TEAM.

You're doing your dream project—who do you need beside you? Bring at least five imaginary people to your leadership group and describe the skills and experience each one of them brings to the team.

Now make a list of the qualities that aren't appropriate for your dream team. For example, you might not be willing to work with people who lose their temper and are verbally abusive when they're stressed or with people who tend not to take responsibility when they've messed up.

2. YOUR SUPPORT CIRCLE.

Who do you call when things get sticky in your life? Whose call will you take, no matter what else is going on, when you know they're going through a difficult time?

This is your support network. (You might also just call them your friends.)

These are the people who know everything about you, that you'll share it all with. And no matter what is going on, they're on your side. Sure, they might call you on your stuff sometimes, but they'll do it in a way that reminds you that they love you whatever it is you're up to.

Just as importantly, you share values. If someone is into gossiping about others and you're committed to not judging or shaming other people, they probably won't be in your support circle even if you love them.

If you're fortunate, your support circle is full. But for most of us, this is a shifting thing throughout our lives. The people we're closest to have babies, or move to different cities, or get too busy with work to make time for the relationship.

For this reason, it's a good idea to be always open to connecting with new people with whom you can develop this kind of connection over time.

**3. YOUR LIFE PARTNER
(AND CHILDREN, POTENTIALLY).**

This list can save you from so much suffering in your life if you make it early enough: write down ten absolutely non-negotiable qualities in your prospective life partner.

We already talked a lot about how you make these connections in your life through the power of play, but unless you know how to recognize your team, your support circle and a potential life partner, you're going to waste a lot of time.

By articulating these qualities, you'll be much quicker to recognize the people that you want in your life—and just as critically, to recognize the people you don't want in your life.

Once you've found your team, your support circle and your life partner, remember that each one of these people (to varying degrees, obvs.) is essential to your well-being. That means that they must be on your nourishment list—the list that you prioritize because, in addition to all the other good reasons, you cannot be completely happy unless they are happy.

Now that you have this information, however, I am here to tell you that there will be times when it is wise to ignore it.

There is no one on the planet who doesn't know something that you don't. While it is wise to be careful about the people you prioritize in your life, the more open you can be to people who are completely different than you, the wiser you will be.

We must make choices to keep moving forward—every yes is also a no, as discussed earlier. But when it comes to people, understanding that every single human being on earth is just as valuable as we are and has just as much to offer frees us in a way that nothing else can.

We're often taught to confuse judging with choosing. We can *choose* team members with positive attitudes without *judging* those who are suffering from clinical depression. We can choose to be with people who value education without judging those who didn't have the same opportunities.

When we are free of that judgement, we're also free of the tendency to compare ourselves to other people, which we've already established is one of the most soul- and energy-draining things we can do.

When we choose the people we prioritize while still recognizing the beauty and brilliance of those we can't, life becomes so rich.

You = Your People

I do not want this conversation to become in any way political, but there is an essential lesson to be learned from recent world leaders about what it means to be part of a team.

You may be the team leader, but you are only as good as the weakest team member and the weakest relationship in that team.

Whether you admire him as a president or not, very few people would argue that Barack Obama is a cool guy. For one thing, his wife and kids really seem to love him. He makes them laugh, he supports them in their vulnerable moments, and he doesn't put himself before them. Even when he was president of the United States, he once introduced himself to an audience only as "Michelle's husband."

For eight years, President Obama grappled with the most challenging, complex and unsolvable problems the world had to offer up. He took office just as the world's economy collapsed during the financial crisis. He faced intractable opposition on every front, and his opposition's members said quite openly that their only objective was to stop him. From doing anything. At all. Racist occurrences skyrocketed, and if that weren't horrible enough, Obama was blamed for fueling racism.

Throughout what to most people would be an unbearable nightmare, he smiled and went to work every morning determined to do his best. He didn't fall into despair or feel sorry for himself. He worked out forty-five minutes a day, six days a week. He had dinner with his family almost every night.

Is he simply the world's most resilient human being? No. According to him, in interviews he's done during and since his time in office, his success and resilience are down to his wife and daughters. He credits them with keeping his ego in check. (Always remember that the ego is the weakest, most brittle part of our psyche). By reminding him that he owed a duty of care to his family, in addition to the duty of care he'd promised the people of America, they helped him create a sense of perspective even when lives were on the line.

Although his hair grew a lot grayer during those eight years, he remained healthy, optimistic and gracious right until the end and then beyond.

In answer to a question asked by Oprah in an interview three years into the presidency, he said that his relationship with his wife Michelle "…is what keeps me sane, what keeps me balanced, what allows me to deal with pressure … she is just my rock. I count on her in so many ways every single day."

According to a study published in 2017 by Carnegie Mellon University, people with supportive spouses were more likely to take on challenges, experiencing greater growth, happiness and well-being afterwards. While our life partners are likely to have the greatest impact on our lives in this way, having a supportive friend group and professional team undoubtedly has a similar impact.

In the White House, Obama was advised by professionals that he had developed relationships with throughout his life—he continues to work happily and successfully with some of those same people today.

In other words, when it comes to relationships, be an Obama. Do not be the kind of person who manipulates others and treats all relationships as a series of transactions. If you do, your wife may slap your hand away when you try to hold hers on national television. And you'll make awful decisions based on the advice of people who are scared to tell you the truth.

Chapter 10

The Power of Why

If you are not driven by something bigger than you, you will not succeed. You need a reason to get up in the morning and do the hard things, often without achieving the results you want.

As humans, we will sometimes doubt ourselves. We will doubt other humans and life itself. We will face failures and wonder if it's worth it to keep on trying, to continue to work so hard when nothing seems to work out.

On those days, we need a reason outside of ourselves to urge us forward. It may be as close to home as supporting our family today or as far away as making sure the children born this year have the best possible education. Whatever it is, that "Why?" will be our superpower on the darkest days.

In the epigraph for *O's Little Guide to Finding Your True Purpose*, Oprah writes, "We're all called. If you're here breathing, you have a contribution to make to our human community. The real work of your life is to figure out your function—your part in the whole—as soon as possible, and then get about the business of fulfilling it as only you can."

I love this quote partly because, if you think about it, it is hard to describe what Oprah does. I mean, it's inarguable that she's had an enormous impact on the world. But is it her interviews? Her presence? Her charitable education work? The deeper conversations she's popularized? [All of it] multiplied by [all of it]?

Oprah would have sold herself short if she believed her purpose was to be the world's most-watched talk show host. Whatever you do, remember that you, too, are likely selling yourself short in terms of your impact. What is the greatest impact you *could* have? Trick question—you won't know until it's all over. Never stop reaching higher.

Canadian entrepreneur and business coach Vivian Kaye breaks it down as simply and clearly as I've seen in the following four questions.

In your notebook, make a new page for each one. In the week to come, please find ten quiet minutes at some point in your day and think about the questions she asks, one at a time.

We've addressed versions of these questions in earlier parts of the book, so I hope you're coming to them now with a greater sense of self-awareness than you started with. But don't be afraid to let your thinking evolve. Like any other superpower, self-knowledge is progressive—it grows as you use it.

1. WHAT MAKES YOU HAPPY?

Think back over your life and list your most joyous moments.

Now break it down. What was it about those moments that made you happy? Think about the big moments and the small ones—your wedding day and your afternoon tea breaks, perhaps. Your yoga classes and the time you won the Grade 4 track and field 100-yard-race. The day you found out your mom's cancer was in remission, and the way you feel when your dog greets you at the door. Nothing is too small or too great to consider and put on your list.

Happiness is not meant to be the place we live, but the moments in which we are re-energized for the next hills on our path. If we recognize this, we will also recognize that our need for happiness is not selfish any more than fueling our bodies to keep on living is selfish.

With this perspective in mind, it becomes easier to identify and seek out those experiences that nourish us.

Many years ago, someone told me that any job or project should fulfill us in at least two of these three ways: financially, in growth and learning, and in enjoyment. Whatever you're doing, if you're not getting two out of the three, it's time to start planning a move.

In looking for our why, we're looking for the intersections. If we are offered a project that pays little but energizes us and in which we learn a lot, that may be the win we need. Other times, we may be primarily driven by the need for a certain income, but we should also look to be growing or enjoying our work. Ideally, of course, we'll be looking for a career that we enjoy, that pays us enough to live in the way we wish to, and in which we're constantly learning.

In *O's Little Guide to Finding Your True Purpose*, in an essay by the French philosopher Alain de Botton, he writes, "… people searching for their aptitudes should act like treasure hunters passing over their lives with metal detectors, listening to beeps of joy."

While it is so useful to ask ourselves these questions here and now, our answers will evolve every day, hopefully for the rest of our lives.

De Botton ends his essay by saying, "We should also consider that, in the end, the answer to 'Who are you meant to be?' is perhaps this: the person who keeps posing the question."

To be fully ourselves, in other words, requires that we regularly reflect on these questions and adjust our course as we change. To do anything else is to sell our future selves short. We cannot know now how much deeper and greater we will be in ten years or twenty, but we can make sure we avoid choices that limit our growth or oppress the future us.

2. WHAT ARE YOUR SKILLS, TALENTS AND EXPERIENCE?

As we've explored earlier, you have a singularly unique gift to give to the world. Right now, you may not have any idea how you'll deliver that gift, but you can begin to figure out what it is.

Start with the activities that come so easily to you they don't feel like work even when you're paid to do them.

For me, it's connecting authentically with others, bringing passion and energy to other people's projects, and understanding how today's technology is changing old ways of doing things. It's also natural for me to think in the biggest possible terms about any project I'm involved with—how can we make this the best it can potentially be and reach the widest audience?

Whether I'm being paid or not, those activities energize me and make me happy.

What are the activities that energize you? What are you most likely to be doing when you experience the state of flow, where an hour can pass like a minute and a day can pass like an hour?

Next, list all the things that people have asked you to do for them or others.

Then list all the things that you have offered to do for other people, whether or not those things relate to the work you're currently being paid to do. Are you the person who offers to set up Grandma's new iPad? The family chef or party planner?

Now list all the skills your studies and experience have equipped you with, everything from, say, making a spreadsheet to knowing the algebra involved in building a rocket. Do you know how to mediate an argument between two four-year-olds? Write that down. That's gold.

Each item on your list is a clue to your why, your reason for being. Just follow your curiosity. It won't let you down, but it will definitely choose the scenic route over the freeway.

3. WHAT IMPACT DO YOU WANT TO MAKE?

It's rare to change the whole world, but we can certainly change our corner of it.

Mother Teresa chose to comfort the suffering in India; Nelson Mandela devoted his life to ending apartheid in South Africa. Martin Luther King Jr. gave his life to ending the plague of racism, even though he knew that the battle would take generations.

For me, it's pretty simple—I want life to be better for those who are younger than me. To make that happen, I want to do everything in my power to provide them with education that really equips them to reach their best possible life. I want to bring passion and energy to all my relationships, personal and professional.

Ask yourself who, what and where:

- who will you impact,
- what will change for them when you do, and
- where will your work make a difference. (Geographically and in terms of societal demographics, such as in the southern U.S. or among low-income children.)

Who needs the skills, experience and talents you have to offer? Where are they? How will you reach them?

4. HOW WILL YOU MEASURE YOUR SUCCESS?

If we wait for other people to tell us how we're doing, we lose ourselves and our connection to our superpowers. Therefore, we must have a way of measuring our progress that doesn't involve the opinions of others.

It might be as simple as asking ourselves each day how close we came to doing our best work—how close we came to showing up as our best self.

It might be your progress toward the series of goals that you mapped out in your action steps. It might be a check-in with your mentors for their feedback on your progress.

Whatever it is, make a note of it, decide how often you'll check in with yourself and how, and then do that thing!

Celebrating the small wins is an important way of nourishing yourself. Course-correcting the losses and missteps is an essential means of getting back on track when things go wrong.

The "Why" payoff

These days, I'm fortunate that many people approach me with lucrative opportunities, deals that could make me very wealthy. I'm not averse to wealth—I love money and what it can do for the people I care about. But because I know my "why," these opportunities are easy to turn down if they don't align with my mission.

One of the world's largest tech companies recently offered me a very high-paying job I knew I'd be great at. I was pleased to be considered, but as we talked, it became evident that their mission is entirely different than mine.

When I told my close friends what they'd offered, I thought they'd think I was crazy to have turned it down. I was ready for some pushback.

I'd forgotten that I've lived from my "why" for many years now, and my friends know and align with that value. Their collective response was more like, "No, of course you wouldn't do that. That's not you at all."

When I met Quincy Jones III, he wasn't trying to accomplish anything other than being genuinely supportive.

Since then, he's continued to be an inspiration to me, but when he reads this book, I'm sure he'll be shocked to find out that, no matter how successful I become, I will think about him as the person who changed everything for me.

In some ways, I am where I am today because of him. But he doesn't think about the influence he has. In his mind, he's just someone who is passionate about storytelling and the power of entertainment to heal, someone who is committed to using his gifts to make the world better.

When you know your why, when you are committed to sharing your gifts authentically and serving others, you will naturally start changing other people's lives.

When I met Quincy, he was just being himself.

The knowledge that our why is about how we serve others is a superpower. From the perspective of our contributions to the world, of course—but also because **this is how we convince our unconscious mind that we are worthy of the lives we aspire to.**

I'm often in situations that scare me to death. I'm nervous. I'm not sure I'll be at my best. But then I remember my why. I remember who I am, and who and what I work for.

I'm never just showing up for me—everything I do is about making a difference for others. Remembering that brings me back to the moment, to just showing up as authentic Gezim.

Does that mean I've always done my best?

Of course not. There is no human alive who could say that—we are connected to each other by our wins and our losses. But if we are committed to serving something bigger than our own wants and needs, we will find strength when we need it.

We will be restored to ourselves.

Your Why and Social Media

Knowing your why has always been a critical element in success, but never more than it is today.

Social media is making people crazy. It's so easy to fall into focusing on engagement numbers and attention, which trigger the ego. As mentioned earlier, our ego is the weakest part of our psyche. It's always afraid, always negative, always scanning the outside world for messages that we're in danger.

When our ego is triggered, we're not present for other people, and we're not our authentic selves.

Yet our ego will always be triggered when we step outside our comfort zones. How do we transcend this catch-22?

By thinking about the people we serve. When I'm outside of my comfort zone, I think about my family—about my nieces and nephews and the opportunities I want for them. I think about my students, the ones I've worked with and those I haven't met yet.

When I do, I remember that my only job is to show up and be myself for them.

If your aim in life is to be "Number One," whatever that means for you, you'll walk a very lonely, dangerous, unhappy road. But if your aim is to help other people, your days will be full of great times with other creators.

I never compete with other people. That's not a good life. My only competition is between the person I was yesterday and the person I know I can be today; between the work I was capable of before and the work I can be capable of in the future.

Acknowledging the Seasons of Your Life

To avoid getting caught up in wanting the success other people have achieved, you must find the peace that comes with accepting that everyone has their own time. We all have great things to do, but this moment may not yet be our time.

It's a cliche to say that we're all where we're supposed to be. Maybe we aren't. Who knows? But what we can be sure of is this: if it isn't happening right now, it isn't our time.

And if we are taking our action steps, moving in the right direction, our time will come.

Being the Best versus Following Your Why

I've met performers who make sure that no one will look better than them, even putting it in their project contracts.

That's one of the reasons we see so many unhappy people in the entertainment industry and in business—they feel they must be "the best." Instead of aiming to be their best selves, they're comparing themselves to others. Even if they reach the top, it's only a matter of time until someone displaces them, so they have to scramble all the time.

The people I've come to admire and learn from are those who want to succeed by doing *their* best and inspiring others.

Giving back is just the best feeling.

It can be as simple as building bridges with other people who share the same mindset, like when I went back to Kosovo to launch a collaboration between our LA institute and Dua Lipa, her dad Dukagjin Lipa and their Sunny Hill Foundation.

It can be going far beyond our commitments to make great things happen for our students at the institute.

To achieve greatness in whatever you do, you must bring greatness to others. Whatever I'm doing, that is where I'm focused—on doing great for others. And that automatically brings me back to my best self. I believe in the domino effect: if you give greatly to others, great things will come to you.

That feeling of deserving great things is so powerful. It is an energy that transmits itself to people around you as a kind of welcoming excitement.

When people talk about charisma, I think this is what they mean: the quality of being absolutely sure that you have something beautiful and valuable to give to other people.

I feel great when I wake up and call my mom and dad to hear their voices and talk to them and when I've spoken to my siblings, nieces and nephews. It makes me feel good.

My family taught me that it is what we give to the people in our lives that makes us happy and strong. Whatever happens, it is the human connections that we share with other people that bring us joy and success.

I've always known my life was bigger than flashy cars and big homes. I think that goes back to my parents. I never got attached to the materialistic stuff. They taught me that true greatness is within reach for all of us.

If you're miserable at any point and you want to feel joy, just figure out how you can make life better for other people and do it.

Chapter 11

Your Mission: Be the Kindest Person in the Room

In several places earlier in the book, I said that I never doubted that I had a special purpose to fulfill with my life. That's true. But there was a time that I didn't believe I'd be able to fulfill that purpose in Sweden.

By the time I was eleven, I knew that I would have a future in the entertainment industry. My gut feeling told me.

I was very inspired by pop. Sweden is the home of ABBA! Swedish songwriters and producers are the most successful in the world; comparatively tiny Sweden is the third-largest exporter of music, after the U.S and the U.K.

Yet I would go to the music store and the names behind the songs were all native Swedish names. I couldn't connect. I felt that people like me, people who weren't blue-eyed and blond-haired and born in Sweden, just didn't have a place in pop music there. I've already mentioned being told I was a "good refugee"—that happened with teachers as well as other kids. What they might have thought of as a compliment made me feel I didn't belong there.

I became convinced that I'd have to leave my family behind and go to Los Angeles. I'd get my start there and there would be no going back.

I finally shared these feelings with the wonderful music teacher I told you about, Harriet, when I was eleven.

She said, "I understand how you could feel that way. I don't blame you. But I need you to stay after school. I want to tell you something."

At the end of the day as I waited for her, I wondered what she would tell me. There was nothing that could make me change my mind. I would succeed, but not in Sweden.

I saw Harriet walking towards me with a big smile and a portfolio, which turned out to be filled with CDs and newspaper article reprints. The next five minutes changed my life forever.

"I want you to know that you can succeed in Sweden," Harriet said. "You can succeed no matter where you're from.

"Don't ever listen to anyone who tells you differently. This is Rami Yacoub," she said, pointing to the back of one of the CDs, "and he is just like you, a Swede with a foreign background. He made it and I know you can too. From now on, I want you to have Rami as an example whenever you feel you can't make it here."

I had to remove my big glasses and catch my breath, because my energy went from zero to 100. Rami Yacoub became my superhero. My eyes and smile were bigger than I ever could remember.

I went home and told my parents, "I have a chance to make it in Sweden!" That night before going to sleep I wrote about it in my school diary.

"Harriet told me about Rami Yacoub today. I think he's really cool. He's my idol."

In 2000-2001, when this happened, Rami Yacoub was already **huge** in the entertainment industry. I hadn't heard of him before Harriet told me about him, but like everyone else, I'd sure heard his music. His first collaboration with legendary Swedish music producer Max Martin was the number one worldwide hit that ignited Britney Spears' career, "Baby One More Time." All the biggest NSYNC and Backstreet Boys songs of the time were his. And when a song was a hit then, it was nothing like today. Radio doesn't have the same impact as it did when I grew up. When a song was a hit at that time, it was played everywhere. Today we have our own playlists and choose what we listen to. Back then, everyone could sing along with each hit song, whether they liked it or not.

What mattered most to me about Rami's success was that he'd done it in Sweden's music industry. He is not blond and blue-eyed, he doesn't have a Swedish name, and as Harriet said, he'd built a tremendously successful career there.

From that time, to me, "Rami Yacoub" meant that you can do whatever you want wherever you are. Whenever I ran into barriers, I told myself that Rami had also faced barriers and had overcome them—I could too.

When MySpace came in, when I was eighteen, I messaged Rami and told him how much his success meant to me. And he took the time to reply.

He said, "I know exactly what you feel. Just believe in yourself—believe that you can do it because you want to do it. Not because someone else tells you that you can. If you believe that success is something that belongs to you, it's going to be yours."

After my cousin died, I was scheduled to attend the Denniz Pop Awards in Stockholm, an event recognizing new talent and honoring the legendary Denniz Pop, who died of cancer 1998.

I didn't feel like going at all but as always, work must be done. My mom said, "Gezim, just go and connect with the nicest person there. You don't need to do anything else."

So I went, and it was a beautiful evening.

I met some nice people, but it was the kind of event at which some of the guests wouldn't talk to some other guests because they weren't successful enough. It was a great experience, because I told myself that I would never make anyone feel like that.

When I went through the crowd at the after party, I saw Rami, who I'd never met in person. I waved, and although he couldn't have known who I was, he made his way over and introduced himself. When I told him that I had reached out to him through MySpace, we had a great conversation that ranged from living in Sweden as non-native Swedes to the music industry at the time.

As we talked, I realized that I'd found the nicest person in the room.

Today Rami is a close friend of mine and I look up to him like an older brother. Ever since that conversation with Harriet, he's been my biggest inspiration. As globally successful as he is, he always made time for this Albanian refugee kid. That might have been partly because we were connected by our immigrant stories, but it's also because Rami is always the nicest person in the room.

When I started working at the music school in Sweden, Rami was the first person I invited to do a master class. I wanted to pass the feeling he gave me onto my students.

When we got the green light for the institute in LA, Rami was the first person outside of my family that I texted the news to. Now he's on our advisory committee.

For many years, whatever success I've had or talent I've found, I text Rami first. It's almost like he has a lucky spell on me. If I tell him something, I just know it's going to go well.

I first reached out because I wanted him to know he'd changed one Albanian boy's life—he wanted to offer inspiration to someone who reminded him of the challenges he'd faced growing up. And since then, we've been able to share full-hearted joy in each other's lives and successes, while offering whatever strength we have to each other when life's challenges arise.

I often talk to Rami about storytelling and how important it is. Now he knows that my storytelling started with him. When Harriet told me about him, I knew I wanted to be someone like him, someone who has an impact on other people through his success. Having a hit song is really nothing compared to making people's lives better through our work.

This book is about unlocking your personal superpowers, not so that you can succeed, although you will—but so that you can be the inspiration for others. Whatever else you do, however else you do it, that's your mission. That's your purpose.

You are here to be what Rami Yacoub has been for me. When some kid reaches out to you, I hope you'll be as generous as he was and respond.

If we're out there doing great things with our lives, it's because people like Rami (and Harriet) have shown us that we can. No one does it alone, without inspiration. We're all dependent on each other that way.

Rami just won a Grammy for "Rain on Me" by Lady Gaga and Ariana Grande. Two decades later, he is still killing it.

When you're connecting authentically, when you're living your superpowers, you aren't just doing it for you. Or even for your family.

You are doing it for everyone who is rising up behind you, looking for your light to show them the way.

Imagine the fulfillment in that. Imagine the joy!

Chapter Forever

In his fabulously titled book, *Full Catastrophe Living*, mindfulness teacher Jon Kabat-Zinn writes about the eight-week mindfulness-based stress reduction course that is taught at the center he established.

In each of the first seven weeks, a series of exercises are assigned. Kabat-Zinn and the rest of the staff refer to the eighth week as "the rest of your life" because it is at that point that the participants must take everything they've learned and turn it into a life practice that never ends.

That, my friends, is where we are today. Enough about me—you now have the tools you need to leverage your own experiences into powerful learning and connecting opportunities like those I've been blessed with.

To start, let's recap in your own words. I've left some space for your notes—don't be afraid to jot down your own aha-moment realizations about these lessons.

Have you claimed your superpowers? If not, what steps are you taking to do that? I've summarized the things you've learned. It's now up to you to integrate them into your life—and to unlock the power of you.

Claiming your superpower of story

You know that you have the power to choose your story, and that once you do, the power of your story can take you anywhere. The only real mistake you can make here is to let other people choose your story for you.

Claiming your superpower of you

You know how to write your story, not just today, but over and over again, incorporating all the elements that make your story a superpower.

Claiming your superpower of moments

You know the power that can only be found in moments, and only then if we are *present* to those moments. You know that creating regular opportunities for reflection and mindfulness in your life is the only way to develop and strengthen this presence over time.

Claiming your superpowers of yes and no

You know that a powerful *yes* is the engine that will empower you to live your best life and contribute your most valuable gifts to the world. You know that a powerful *no* is the guardian of that power because each yes is also a no, and each no is also a yes. This knowledge will make each decision in your life a two-part exercise: what are you saying yes to, and what are you saying no to at the same time.

Claiming your superpower of a dream

You know how to turn your dream into the inevitable destination of the path of least resistance by:

- creating a powerful, detailed vision,
- writing an honest, thorough current reality statement, and
- then mapping your action steps and breaking them down into SMART goals.

Claiming your superpower of play and passion

You know the power of play and passion in creating, in recharging yourself for long-term success, and for connecting with others and building community. You know the activities that fuel you, and you've started scheduling more time in your life to play.

Claiming your superpower of authentic connection

You know the power of authenticity and vulnerability and that these abilities are the only sustainable way to connect with your life partner, your professional team, your support circle and your community. You know how to let go of what other people might think of you or feel about you so that you can show up as your whole self whatever the circumstances. You know that who you know is far less important than the kind of relationship you have with them.

Claiming your superpower of resilience

You know how to bounce back from hard times and find the treasure in the hard lessons that life presents you with.

Claiming your superpower of creative collaboration

You know how to identify and connect with your people. You know that prioritizing and nurturing those important relationships is as important as eating well and getting enough sleep.

Claiming the superpower of your why

You know your why, and you know why it is essential to reflect on your why and update it regularly.

There's your toolkit, my friend, your ten-pack of superpowers. With it, there is absolutely nothing that can stop you.

I hope to see you out there in the arena, living your best life and changing the world. And in the meantime, feel free to send me your stories and let me know how your superpowers are working for you.

You know where to find me.

References

Brené Brown, Ph.D.
Rising Strong: The Reckoning. The Rumble. The Revolution
Random House 2015

Stuart Brown, M.D. and Christopher Brown
Play: How it Shapes the Brain, Opens the Imagination, and Invigorates the Soul
Avery 2010

Susan Cain
Quiet, The Power of Introverts in a World that Can't Stop Talking
Penguin 2013

James Clear
Atomic Habits: An Easy & Proven Way to Build Good Habits & Break Bad Ones
Penguin Random House 2018

Pema Chödrön
When Things Fall Apart: Heart Advice For Difficult Times
Shambala 1996

Stephen R. Covey
The 7 Habits of Highly Effective People
Free Press 1989

Robert Fritz
The Path of Least Resistance: Learning to Become the Creative Force in Your Own Life
Random House 1989

Adam Grant
Originals: How Non-conformists Move The World
Penguin Publishing Group 2017

Eric Greitens
Resilience: Hard-Won Wisdom for Living a Better Life
Mariner's Books 2016

Dag Hammarskjöld
Markings
Publisher: Alfred A Knopf 1964

Sam Harris
Waking Up: A Guide to Spirituality Without Religion
Simon & Schuster 2014

Carl Jung
Memories, Dreams, Reflections
Random House 1963
(Copyright expired—now available as a PDF on docsGoogle.com.)

The Editors of O, The Oprah Magazine
O's Little Guide to Finding Your True Purpose
Flatiron Books 2015

Peace Pilgrim
Peace Pilgrim: Her Life and Work in Her Own Words
(A compilation of her writings published by her friends after her death.)
Ocean Tree Books 1992
(Available free of charge from her website: https://www.peacepilgrim.org/to-receive-free-peace-pilgrim-book.)

Marsha Sinetar
Do What You Love, the Money Will Follow: Discovering Your Right Livelihood
Dell 1986

Guy Winch, Ph.D.
Emotional First Aid: Healing Rejection, Guilt, Failure, and Other Everyday Hurts
Penguin Random House 2013

Acknowledgements

Thank you to my family for being the biggest support I could ever ask and for being there for me no matter what. There are no words to ever explain how much I love you. I'm proud to be your son, brother and uncle. Ju dua pa fund.

Thank you to each of you who made a big impact on my journey in Sweden and in the United States, especially Grönkullaskolan in Alvesta, Sweden, Harriet, Gittan, Gunilla Hellgren, Joe Labero, Kungsmadskolan in Växjö, Anders Rydholm, Per Svensson, Magnus Sundholm, and all my students from Sweden.

I am so grateful to the OCS IAI team in Westlake Village, California: Head of School, Rob Black, Dr. Matt Northrop, Mary Kay Altizer, Dr. Jim Altizer, Edward Rouse, Lauren Hemsworth, Rosalind Enciso, Andrew Christopher, Anna Wadman, and Caitlin Phillips.

Thank you to the OCS IAI Advisory council for believing in us: Alyssa Lein-Smith, Jimmy "Jam" Harris, James Burnett, Ulla Sjöstrom, Ryan O'Quinn, Kristoffer Polaha, Alan Carter, Jordyn Palos, Joey Scott and Rami Yacoub.

And to everyone who has changed my life but who would prefer to remain unnamed ... you know who you are.

To my amazing publishing team ... love you!

To my book editor, Lori Bamber: Your guidance, support and mindset have been extremely valuable, and our conversations have been memories of a lifetime. No matter what happens when I release the book, I'm forever thankful I can say, "We did this together."

To my project manager, Megan Watt: Megan, thank you for being a boss, for always answering my questions and for making this process so easy. You are a powerful human being and I respect and appreciate you a lot. Thank you for believing in me.

To my brand author, Anna Mullens: Anna, Anna, Anna, where do I start? It's very rare to connect and share incredible energy the way we have since day one. You are someone I see as a dear friend, and I know we will continue to collaborate for many years. You are incredible, and a storyteller who is so important for our future. Thank you for always being there.

To my book designer, Jazmin Welch: Jazmin, we did it! I knew we were going to create my dream cover. You made it happen. Thank you for being so understanding, for trying to see things from my point of view and for always having a smile on your face. I'm so proud to have you as a friend.

Gezim Gashi is a storyteller, producer, mentor, speaker, educationalist, branding guru and a partner in the OCS Institute for the Arts & Innovation in Los Angeles, California. This is his first book. Originally from Akllap, Kosovo, he grew up in Alvesta, Sweden and now lives in New York City and California.

To my nephews and nieces:
DREAM BIG!

Always yours, Uncle Gezim

Printed in Great Britain
by Amazon